Writing and the Spirit

How to Change the World

KEN KUHLKEN

PRAISE FOR WRITING AND THE SPIRIT

"The themes of Ken Kuhlken's vignettes kept drawing me in: being humble in writing, being generous with giving yourself away, getting quiet in order to write, and how to create a masterpiece that will change someone's life." — Philip Yancey, award-winning author of over 20 books, including *Where Is God When It Hurts?* and *What's So Amazing about Grace?* philipyancey.com

---

"In *Writing and the Spirit,* Ken Kuhlken speaks with all the ease of a friend on your couch. An ingenius, multiple-PhD-holding, wise-man sort of friend, if you have one of those. His observations from the world about us, writers in history and his own experience (failures and triumphs) combine to form an insightful, relevant work for all writers of faith.

"He examines the (inner and outer) confrontations all writers must engage with in order to produce meaningful work. Among them are the nature of inspiration, imagination, and how not to be a hack. He also covers the downright nitty-gritty of the thing — the practical conditions that we all strive for and against in order to produce works in which, as he's noted elsewhere, 'the words sing'.

"This is an all-around handbook of writerly wisdom that anyone who hopes to change the world must read." — Anastasia Campos, writer and photographer. anastasiacampos.com

ALSO BY KEN KUHLKEN

Novels
Midheaven

Tom Hickey California Crime novels
The Biggest Liar in Los Angeles
The Good Know Nothing
The Venus Deal
The Loud Adios
The Angel Gang
The Do-Re-Mi
The Vagabond Virgins

Memoir
Reading Brother Lawrence

With Alan Russell
Road Kill
No Cats, No Chocolate

On Writing
Write Smart

ISBN: 978-0-9759047-6-3

BISAC: LAN005000 LANGUAGE ARTS &
DISCIPLINES / Composition & Creative Writing

Published by
HICKEY'S BOOKS
www.hickeybooks.com

An enterprise of
PERELANDRA COLLEGE
8697-C La Mesa Boulevard, PMB 21
La Mesa, California 91942
www.perelandra.edu

Table of Contents

one — I'm an Artist and So are You

Who and What is an Artist?

"We are God's art, created in Christ Jesus to do works of beauty, which God has prepared in advance for us to do." Ephesians 2:10

"So God created mankind in his own image ... male and female ..." Genesis 1:27.

We are made in the image of the master artist, the creator of all creation, to create works of beauty.

Though we may not be called to quit our day jobs, run off to Tahiti and paint our impressions of the islanders, we are meant to view our work and our lives from an artist's perspective.

Whether our goal is to provide announcements for a church newsletter, to make of our home a refuge from the storm outside, to save stories and lessons from our lives, to create happiness by loving well, or to compose a novel or film masterpiece, we are called to approach those projects with attitudes guided by the motive of creating works of beauty.

God Is love. Love Is truth. Truth Is Beauty.

John Keats, in "Ode On a Grecian Urn", wrote "Beauty is truth, truth beauty, that is all you know on earth, and all you need to know."

Real beauty, whether in the eye of the creator or the beholder, is an expression of love.

Christ insists, "Let your light shine before men in such a way that they may see your good works [works of beauty] and glorify your father who is in heaven."

We are created in the image of God so that we can make art of and through our lives so that our art can draw people to God. And because God is love, we can draw people to God by helping them love better, which is best accomplished by loving them better.

In my novel The Good Know Nothing detective Tom Hickey and his sister Florence, who works for evangelist Aimee Semple McPherson, are on a road trip when she asks:

"Tommy, do you want to know why I fell for God?"

"Sure."

"It's all your fault," she said.

"How so?"

"See, when you really know love, when you find yourself being truly loved, you can't help thanking God."

A tiny sob issued out of her. Then she scooted closer and kissed her brother's cheek. Tom sat speechless, wondering if his heart might explode.

Florence rode with her head on her brother's shoulder. As distant headlights approached, she said, "The thing is, when you truly thank God, you sort of feel him smile. Then you fall for him. That's all."

About Getting Rich

Buddy Meeker caught me on the way into our church. He led me back outside and said, "Here's a thought. Golf is like life. I mean, one day your game sucks, but it doesn't mean you won't have a great game next time. Or, one day you're on. You think you've mastered the swing. But the next day, you—"

"Suck," I said.

"Right."

I decided not to dampen Buddy's enthusiasm about his discovery by pointing out a theory of mine: most things, if observed closely, can be metaphors for most other things.

In accord with that theory, I'm hoping readers will translate my thoughts about writing in particular to also apply to painting, surfing, cooking, gardening, sewing. To almost anything except getting rich.

From *Citizen Kane*:

Thompson: He made an awful lot of money.

Bernstein: Well, it's no trick to make a lot of money ... if all you want ... is to make a lot of money.

Neither art, nor beauty, nor love, nor truth, are about making money. "For the love of money is the root of all kinds of evil." 1 Timothy 6:10

In a masterful essay, "Forgotten Beauty", novelist Athol Dickson lists the sources of beauty in a story as "deep contemplation, honesty, intentionality, originality and love," And he reminds us that we can't serve two masters. "Write for pride or money, and you do not write for love or beauty."

I have managed to support myself and a family for lots of years by writing and teaching writing. Still, I'm hardly the bestseller some writers dream of becoming. Yet writing has been adventure I wouldn't trade for a majority share of Microsoft.

As most earnest writers would agree, we write because we have to. We get depressed when we don't. Something tells us to write down what we see, feel or imagine. After we've followed that direction, something tells us, "Develop that more, you haven't told the whole story." When we ask, "What's the whole story?" something says "You're only going to learn that by telling it, and telling it well."

In the end, when we've created a story or poem or essay that seems to transcend what we know and what we intended we probably feel closer to the joy God knows in creation than anybody other than creators can feel.

Maybe the something that requires some of us to write, some of us to invent software, some of us to bring loving harmony to our homes and communities, is what we Christians call the Holy Spirit.

A Masterpiece?

Long ago, in Chico, California, I was with students in a taco shop after a creative writing class I taught at the state university a few blocks away.

A student, a black-haired beauty incongruously nicknamed Mord, said, "Writing is so hard, I wonder if it's worth our time to maybe spend our whole lives writing stories and maybe not make any money with them.

"Why do *you* do it?" she asked.

"I have this dream," I said, "that if I write enough stories and work hard enough on them, one of them will be a masterpiece."

"Okay, but how will you know it's a masterpiece?"

"Maybe I won't," I said. "But somebody who reads it might tell me it moved them to have a better life, or to see the world more clearly."

Later, in Tucson, Arizona, Jonathon Penner, a writer and professor, asked, "How do you think we can draw the distinction between art and commercial or hack writing?"

I thought a while and said, "Beats me." But over the years I've discovered a better response.

Art, I'll contend, isn't the creation but the process of giving all our powers to make a creation as superb and honest as we can. The creation may become what we call great art, good art, poor art, or lousy art. But art it is, if the creator gave it his or her all.

And our powers aren't only about innate talent or developed skill, I'm convinced. The most crucial power we have, the one that can make our efforts transcend our talent and skill and give birth to a masterpiece, is the power to get inspired.

Inspired?

For several years I attended a church where people would occasionally stand (or remain sitting) and bring a prophetic word. I suspect the inspiration they receive that prompts these outbursts may be of identical substance to the inspirations that seem to compel us writers to feel what people call "in the zone," as if the words we write are coming from elsewhere.

I was having lunch with Charlie Gregg, a pastor and pastor's kid. He's witnessed probably thousands of what church folks call "words of knowledge" and also written plenty of sermons and devotions. He agreed with my comparison and added, "I feel most convinced that the promptings are from God when I'm in worship."

Perhaps that's a universal experience. If so, and if we could all find a worshipful (thankful and open-hearted) attitude to write within, we'd likely be more open to the Spirit's instructions.

Morty Sklar founded a publishing venture called *The Spirit That Moves Us.*

For those who prefer not to use the word Holy, that's the spirit I mean.

What follows is simply a collection of thoughts about ways to help an artist to spend more time "in the zone," when we feel as if we're given the words rather than digging them out of minds hard as caliche.

Since I get to be the writer, I'm going to use words that apply to my vocation and my vision of how the universe works. But I invite readers to translate into the vocabulary of their own vision. Perhaps the words will ring truer.

*

The Current State of Christian Art

On ChristianityToday.com, I read: "I've puzzled over a riddle for some time now. It goes like this: Those who call on Jesus for salvation are given the Holy Spirit. It's through the Spirit's power that we, simple jars of clay, are able to shine golden and do wonderful things beyond our human capability. So, why do Christians, who claim access to the original creator, so often produce poor art?"

One reason may be that Christians tend not to value their imaginations as much as they value order and discipline. Art can be messy.

When I start to pray, after a few seconds, my mind drifts, and the prayer gets left behind. I've tried meditating. My mind refuses to shut down, or even relax. Now, "prayer warriors" and avid pursuers of meditation would no doubt assure me that practice would bring control over my wandering mind. But so far I haven't felt God urging me to dedicate myself to lengthy prayers or daily meditation. I have, though, sensed him telling me to write most every day.

Even in church, when my thoughts shoot off into some story of mine, often I encounter so many ideas, it's all I can do not to rush out of church and home to my computer.

My poet friend Olga Savitsky spent plenty of church time scribbling.

Maybe the typical artist is like my daughter Darcy, who was diagnosed with ADD. She has uncanny powers of concentration when pursuing anything that excites her. Otherwise, she tends to scatter.

I suspect some of us were created to scatter more readily, to be more self-propelled than other folks, and to resist imposed structures. So, maybe our best road for inching or rushing closer to God is the same road that will lead us toward better paintings, songs or stories. Maybe, since God appears to have designed us to make art, we'll never find peace or please God any other way.

Or maybe I'm nuts.

Let Go and Let God Write

Once more, let's ask, "Why do Christians, who claim access to the original creator, so often produce poor art?"

When Darcy was sixteen, she got into trouble. As a parent, I will of course report that it wasn't her fault, except that she hadn't chosen her friends wisely.

Still, we needed to appear in juvenile court. She was in danger of losing her driver's license for two years and possibly facing harsher penalties. And I believed when she told me that getting busted had "scared her straight."

A friend reminded me that when we aree brought before the authorities, we are not supposed to worry, since the Holy Spirit will teach us what to say. He was thinking of Luke 12:11-12: "When you are brought before synagogues, rulers and authorities, do not worry about how you will defend yourselves or what you will say, for the Holy Spirit will teach you at that time what you should say." Now, whether that verse was meant to apply to me in that situation, who knows?

But when my turn to talk came, I orated a defense that would've convinced Clarence Darrow to hire me as his attorney. Outside, with the charges dropped, Darcy and her brother gawked at me and one of them said, "Wow, Dad." Which I rarely heard when my big kids were teenagers.

My point is, in whatever we writers create, in a sense we are appearing before the rulers and authorities, and liable to find ourselves assisted in our work by the Holy Spirit. But only if we can get our timid and programmed selves out of the way.

two — Mysteries Solved

What in the World is Inspiration?

A fellow named John, perhaps John the disciple, gets a revelation, a series of visions. As he believes the revelation has come by way of an angel, he writes down his visions.

I'm recreating the town of Mount Shasta, California forty years before I first saw it, and the layout of the town comes to me. Later, a woman who has read the book writes and tells me she lived in Mount Shasta during that time, and she wonders how I got it exactly right.

A novel I've labored over most of my adult life, and as of yet haven't finished revising, still calls me to go back and fix it, though I've been willing to let other manuscripts stay on the shelves for eternity.

Richard Shelton is sitting atop his roof when the phone rings. He's expecting an important call, so he starts to climb down but slips and falls into a tree, which breaks his fall. He scurries out of the tree and runs into the house but misses the phone call, and in a flash, a whole poem comes to him. He writes it down and submits it to *The New Yorker*. They publish it. Years later, he can still say it was the only poem he has written that he didn't revise.

When I tell stories about my relatives and other people I know, I get comments like "How come you get to meet all the interesting people?"

One reason I like to use people I have known as the beginnings of characters I fictionalize, is that so many people I have known intrigue me. People we meet can be gifts from the Spirit.

Gifts from the Spirit may include such occurrences as confidence that although we haven't a clue where the story is headed, it will find its way and lead us to some event that brings the previous stuff together. Even words, images or lines that spring to mind most unexpectedly may be gifts from the Spirit.

What Else Might the Spirit Give Us?

Most obviously the Spirit may give us lines that are either clearly or subtly profound and perhaps original, such as Dimitri Karamazov's, "Only how is man going to be good without God? That's the question. I always come back to that. For whom is man going to love then? To whom will he be thankful?" That inspired question given to Feodor Dostoyevski resonated in my thoughts for weeks.

And the Spirit might give us metaphors, such as Olga Savitsky so frequently employed. Here's one I'll probably never forget: "Puny faith is like a rusty zipper."

Maybe even some nonsense comes from the Spirit, to lighten our hearts, such as Lewis Carroll's "Kaloo kaley, we'll eat today like cabbages and kings."

The Spirit may help us with structure or guide us to the right place in our story to use a certain thought or image, so that it can achieve the greatest impact.

The Spirit may even provide a theme or epic narrative that will define our life's work.

William Butler Yeats proposed that for each of us there may exist one archetypal story or explanatory myth that, being understood, might clarify all we do and think, and so explain our destiny.

My friend Genie, a financial advisor, has found the archetype for her life story in the Biblical account of the trials and triumphs of Joseph. In that story she finds guidance, hope and confidence.

Some writers have believed they were given every word, that they were merely channels of a divine or supernatural voice. William Blake was one of these. Many people believe that this method is where Scripture came from.

Inspiration can include whatever makes us feel guided, given directions or clues that seem to come out of nowhere.

I had recently finished *The Loud Adios*, with no intention of it becoming part of a series. I took my kids on vacation, to Lake Tahoe, and we stopped on the way to pick up their friends in Chico, where we used to live.

We stayed in a single motel room. One morning we went horseback riding. After lunch we rented a jet ski. Then the girls wanted to go to a casino arcade and the boys wanted me to take them fishing. I said, "Enough. We're going to hang out in the motel for a couple hours. I need a little rest."

What, rest in a motel room with four kids of any age? These four being adolescents, between spats and teasing and wrestling and feuds over possession of the TV, I only lasted about twenty minutes. Then I decided to risk paying for the damage those barbarians would do. I snuck out and went for a walk on the beach.

I agree with Mark Twain, who wrote of the Tahoe region, "This is the air the angels breathe." I wasn't a hundred yards up the beach before the one book became suddenly part of a series, as the ideas for the next two books came to me, out of nowhere.

Long ago, I was writing on a Sears typewriter that needed cleaning. The main character of a novel I called *Yanqui* was a young baseball player name Skinner. I had finished the whole first draft and was reading it over before I noticed that the sticky "k" had gotten fainter and fainter until the character's name wasn't Skinner, but sinner.

I was going through an awful time. The worst ever. I had lost forty pounds (which would be okay now, but back then I started where losing forty pounds now would leave me). I couldn't sleep more than a couple hours a night, my mind was always roiling, I had a perpetual stomachache. My friend Charlie Morgan, a psychologist, raved in a letter about a book called *The Road Less Travelled*. He knew nothing about my condition. He hadn't meant to help what ailed me. I had entirely forgotten about the recommendation when I went to a B. Dalton's hoping to find a book about relaxation for alleviating sleep disorders. I didn't find one, but noticed the subtitle of a book that equated emotional health with spiritual growth.

Some truths that book proposed turned my life around, started my healing. The book was *The Road Less Travelled*. And I didn't realize until weeks later that it was the book Charlie had recommended.

I subscribe to A Word A Day, a vocabulary-building program that arrives by email. Along with vocabulary building, he offers a quote every day. One quote, from the novelist Paul Auster, rang true and a phrase from it jumped out. Not only did I know instantly that it would be the title of my novel in progress, of which I had already written half, but I recognized that the phrase expressed exactly what the primary theme of the novel should be.

Spirit or Imagination?

Most of us writers don't feel as sure as did William Blake that our every word from God. We also rely on imagination.

I'm not convinced distinguishing between imagination and inspiration is critical to our art or our lives, but it could be, so let's pursue the question.

In a lecture entitled "Imagination vs. Inspiration," poet Garcia Lorca maintained that the imagination was a form of logic that could do many things but couldn't "touch the darker forces of nature or the most incandescent light, or the realm of the unknown." Imagination, he explained, always works with facts borrowed from the "most clear and precise form of reality."

In my experience, imagination usually begins with connections. I build Juan out of character traits I've witnessed. Then I lock Juan in a broken elevator with Lucy, who may have red hair, and I watch what happens. If it charms or excites me, I write it down.

Or a taste reminds me of a hamburger stand named Jub's my friend Eric Curtis and I used to frequent. Soon I'm writing a scene that happens in Mission Beach, where Jub's was located.

That's imagination.

But inspiration appears out of nowhere. Or from somewhere we can't locate. Those who insist upon scientific explanations suppose it arises from deep in our brains. Others of us prefer to credit the Holy Spirit. Whatever the source or path, it manifests itself in moments that can make us gasp in awe of a truth we hadn't noticed before.

And it often gives the kind of truth we can't express in any other terms than the one we've just encountered. A cloud, a mountain, or a child seen from a new angle or in more vivid color. A renewed hope or dedication. A deeper love that, if we try to analyze, vanishes as it returns to where it came from, beneath, beyond or above our reality.

It may be the kind of truth we find so often in the Bible. The kind that comes clear yet remains a mystery.

Angels and Demons

An anecdote about the German poet Rainer Maria Rilke tells of his being invited by his friend the psychologist Karl Jung to undertake psychotherapy. Rilke declines the offer, saying "I'm afraid if my demons go, my angels will go with them."

In legend and literature are a host of characters who have bartered with the devil and traded their souls for creative powers.

William Blake, especially in "The Marriage of Heaven and Hell," portrays the angelic and the demonic as equally powerful and necessary. A Christian reading Blake may wish he could ask the poet, "Hey, which side are you on?"

Blake might explain that he roamed like a foreign correspondent through the spirit world, in the midst of a heavenly battleground, surrounded by firefights and war cries, reporting on what he saw and heard. He may have simply felt called to write what he witnessed and leave judgment to his readers.

Suppose a spirit gives us strange words, wild combinations of words, lines rich with meanings we have never consciously meant, and suppose they make us feel wicked, cruel or severely deranged, in a fearful way.

Just because inspiration strikes doesn't mean we're obliged to accept it. Perhaps Hitler was inspired to massacre, Eric Rudolph to bomb abortion clinics. My friend Tony, who is schizophrenic, hears voices that command him to curse at apparently innocent people.

The Spirit that moves us toward God and/or the good doesn't hold a monopoly.

We artists are called to attend to inspiration, not to be any spirit's pawns.

More Angels and Demons

Edward Hirsch's book *The Demon and the Angel* is devoted to enlightening us about the spirit that moves us, often through the insights of master writers.

Hirsch reports that Ralph Waldo Emerson wrote in his *Journals,* "Blessed is the day when the youth discovers that Within and Above are synonyms."

He informs us that Garcia Lorca referred to the spirit he sought, so that he could ask it to inhabit his poems, as the *duende.* He believed the *duende* was associated with the spirit of earth, visible anguish, irrational desire and enthusiasm, and a fascination with death. He held that the *duende* will not come unless he sees death is possible.

Writers seeking Lorca's *duende* ought to heed an admonition of Master Jeong, under whom I studied Tae Kwon Do. "Don't fight unless you're willing to die."

I'd like to know whether Lorca's *duende* is a spirit of creation or of destruction. Czeslaw Milosz might ask the same question. Milosz, who attests that poems are dictated to him by the spirit, concludes his *ars poetica* "with the hope/that good spirits, not evil ones, choose us for their instrument."

I'm convinced that both good and evil spirits exist. Hirsch quotes poet Charles Simic (from *Dime-Store Alchemy: The Art of Joseph Cornell*), "...one needs to believe in angels and demons even in a modern world in order to make sense of it." And Simic declares, "Making art in America is about saving one's soul." I would scratch "in America," insert "on earth" in its place. I would argue that the mythic conflict the Faust legend presents, in which a creative person meets with the temptation to exchange his soul for powers granted by the devil, is a theme present in each of our lives.

Perhaps blues singer Robert Johnson as well as Friedrich Nietzsche, Garcia Lorca, the Marquis de Sade and Charles Baudelaire got inspired by the spirit that granted Faust's wish. Then the *duende* could be another name for what Dostoyevski's Ivan Karamazov calls "the dread spirit."

In *The Brothers Karamazov*, Satan is talking to Ivan. "Listen, in dreams and especially in nightmares, from indigestion or anything, a man sometimes sees such artistic visions, such complex and real actuality, even a whole world of events, woven into such a plot, with such unexpected details from the most exalted matters to the last button on a cuff, as I swear Leo Tolstoy could not create."

Artists can get addicted to such visions. Emerson confessed, "The one thing which we seek with insatiable desire is to forget our selves, to be surprised out of our propriety, and to do something without knowing how or why."

W.B. Yeats believed spirits need us as much as we need them. He agreed with Irish folk tradition that the spirit may offer us wisdom but only humans can deliver the wisdom. Which implies the same spirit (or spirits) we're looking to access is looking to access us.

Maybe all us artists are possessed.

What Would Jesus Do?

Jesus would tell a story.

When my son Cody was fourteen and more troubled than I can write about and keep from feeling my heart break all over again, I gave him a Bible. I had only recently begun attending church. Sometimes Cody would go with me, but though he would never admit to being baffled, I sensed he didn't have the background required to take much from the messages. So I bought him a Bible of his own and suggested that if he read at least Matthew and Acts, he'd get some basics that would make church less strange and tedious.

Late that night, he ran upstairs. Sounding more animated than he had in a couple of years, he said, "Hey, I thought this Bible was a lot of preaching, but it's a great story."

According to the 1965 film, it is *The Greatest Story Ever Told*?

e*

In his essay "Faith and Fiction," novelist Fredrick Buechner contends that whether what we call inspiration comes from the Holy Spirit, from the muse (who or whatever she may be), or results from a lucky break in the process of imagining, it's possible at least every now and then to be better than we are, to write more than we know. And he points out that St. Paul asked, "Do you not know that God's spirit dwells in you?"

And 1 Corinthians 2:16 maintains, "But we have the mind of Christ." Which could mean that Christ's mind has entered ours, thereby giving us its capabilities. Or it could mean that we can use our minds in the same ways Christ used his.

Either interpretation tells me we are capable of tuning in and getting divine help with our stories, essays or landscaping. And if we aren't tuning in, if the Spirit isn't helping, the problem may lie with our attitude.

One Sunday Gary Goodell, a pastor and former seminary professor, proposed that it may be through the act of communion that Christ enters our being.

Let's suppose this is the case. Then having the mind of Christ depends upon receiving communion, and according to 1 Corinthians 11: 23-29, receiving communion (rather than just gobbling and swilling) requires a humble and honest attitude.

So, attitude may be the key to the place (or places) the Spirit (or spirits) rests. Our attitude may determine which spirit can move us, as well as how much we hear of what the Spirit has to say.

three — Attitude is Almost Everything

Begin With The Spirit

When I moved back to my hometown of San Diego from Chico, California, I left behind a tenured professorship. My kids lived with me and cost plenty. So I started teaching all around.

One semester, I was teaching nine classes at four colleges, putting in about ninety hours a week, which left me too weary to write, or so I thought.

Also, Cody and I attended Tae Kwon Do classes twice a week. And I was managing Cody's Little League team, hoping he might become a pitcher instead of a ninja.

Probably because I didn't sleep enough, my emotions had shut down. I couldn't even feel dread or anger while driving the freeways. Something had to change. My kids didn't deserve a catatonic dad.

One late afternoon as I sat on the grass at the University of San Diego, overlooking the harbor and wondering how I could repair my emotions, I mumbled, "Okay, where should I start?"

Then I remembered advice Master Jeong, our Tae Kwon Do instructor, often gave. He told us, "Everything begins with the spirit. From the spirit come the thoughts. From the thoughts come the actions. From the actions come the habits. From the habits comes the character. And from the character comes the destiny."

Stupefied by stress as I was, I sat a while wondering where on that continuum I should start trouble-shooting, until the obvious made itself clear.

Start with the spirit.

So, I thought, what could best set my spirit on the right path?

I believe it was God who sent the message: "Look here, you're a writer. But for months you haven't been writing, which has grieved your spirit into a coma. Sure, teaching nine classes and raising kids is hard, but it's not going to kill you. What will kill you is not writing."

The next morning, I got up at 5 a.m. instead of 5:30, which allowed me to write for a half hour. Not much, but enough to give me the hope that comes when our lives feel in motion toward a better place. And hope is the antidote to despair.

The stuff I wrote during those half-hour sessions became crucial parts of my novel *The Loud Adios*. About a month after the semester ended, I sent the manuscript to a national contest.

I won.

Which meant I earned enough so I didn't need to teach as much and, after too many discouraging years, I would see a new novel of mine on bookstore shelves.

Which can be an inspiring sight.

Get Real

I'll turn this thought over to a couple fellows brighter than I'll ever be.

SØren Kierkegaard wrote, "A person with originality comes along, and consequently does not say: one must take the world as it is, but: whatever the world may be, I remain true to my own originality, which I do not intend to change according to the good pleasure of the world. The moment that word is heard, there is as it were a transformation in the whole of existence, as in the fairy story--when the word is said the magic castle, which has been under a spell for a hundred years, opens again, and everything comes to life. In the same way existence becomes all eyes. The angels grow busy, look about with curiosity to see what is going to happen, for that is what interests them. On the other side, dark and sinister demons, who have sat idle for a long while gnawing their fingers, jump up, stretch their limbs: 'This is something for us,' they say.

"This is what the apostle means when he says that the Christian's fight is not merely against flesh and blood but with principalities and powers."

Friedrich Nietzsche, whom I consider the most influential philosopher of the modern age, contends that while peoples' most common and dominant quality is laziness their second most common and dominant quality is a kind of nervous fear. He argues that what they fear most is the trouble refusing to conform and exposing who they truly are would cause them. So, he admonishes, "Become who you are," which I will repeat again and again. Because the acceptance of that message and devotion to the principal can launch a process that will change everything, for the better.

Like knowing Olga Savitsky changed many of us.

In church, Olga read poems of hers she felt God wanted us to hear. She believed God gave her the poems, as did William Blake and no doubt vast numbers of us writers too afraid of appearing ridiculous to admit that belief.

Olga's poems are rough. She didn't studied poetry writing or even read much poetry beyond those assigned in high school. In college, she didn't major in literature or writing. Yet inspired lines leapt out of her poetry and grabbed us. I suspect the Spirit entered her poems because above all, she meant them to be honest expressions of her heart.

My dad died when I was young, so I don't recall much of his wisdom. But one piece I remember is: "If you want a girl to fall for you, don't try to impress her, just be yourself." I often pass along that advice, only not about winning girls, but about making art.

Each of us is more unique than we have ever suspected. But we've been taught to conform, in actions, language, ideas, and even desires and daydreams. If there exists on earth a culture that isn't structured toward creating conformity I'd like to know about it.

Now and then, someone breaks through the programming, discovers whom she is and lives as her real self, and we either view her with amazement, or with suspicion, or we send the police or the church ushers to restrain her.

A few writers impress me as being so original we have reason to wonder if they came from another planet or another reality. Franz Kafka, SØren Kierkegaard, Flannery O'Connor, and Olga come to mind as such masters at being themselves.

Though I may never find my original self to the degree they did, or even dare to expose what parts of me I do find, I'm convinced that to the extent I can be real, honest and true to myself, at least while writing, people will read and value my stories.

Get Tough

Aside from admonishing us to become who we are, Nietzsche warns us that creators must be hard and courageous.

One of the artist's tasks is to show how unique people really are, what a wonder each of us is. And the most fruitful means to reveal the truth about people is to risk giving the truth about ourselves.

To encourage the timid, Nietzsche offers, "The secret of the greatest fruitfulness and the greatest enjoyment of existence is: to *live dangerously.*" Besides, he assures us, artists can take solace in knowing they have molded the future like wax. Which Nietzsche most surely did, by championing the rise of a superman (which Hitler picked up and ran with) and by proclaiming that "God is dead."

By "God is dead," he simply meant that people no longer act as if God existed, making God essentially irrelevant. Using that same logic, we must be able to bring God back to life.

In his work on myth, Joseph Campbell advises us to follow our bliss and promises that if we do so without fear, doors will open where we didn't even know doors existed. He reminds us that in the story of Sir Galahad, "the knights agree to go on a quest, but thinking it would be a disgrace to go forth in a group, each 'entered into the forest, at one point or another, where they saw it to be thickest, all in those places where they found no way or path.'"

Where we see a path, it's someone else's path. So: "Each knight enters the forest at the most mysterious point and follows his own intuitions. What each brings forth is what never before was on land or sea: the fulfillment of unique potentialities, which are different from anybody else's."*

Loathe B.S.

When I told Olga that if we started a church, we should hang a sign over the door "No B.S.", she said, "Do we have to use the initials?"

A friend I know very well, a Christian who was fairly new to churchgoing, found himself dating a woman who didn't believe in God or much else except romance and money. But she was smart and witty and one of the sexiest females imaginable. I met her. She was built like a playmate, had a lovely, kind face and baby- fresh skin. My friend hoped that sooner or later she would turn to believing close enough to the way he did so they might consider marriage.

Meanwhile, my friend was being mentored by an older and more experienced Christian. When he told the mentor that he was having a tough time because every date, the woman tried to seduce him, the mentor commented that his effort to resist was remarkable. Out of many such cases the mentor had known about, my friend was the only man who resisted very long.

Rather than making him feel heroic, the comment discouraged him, because it seemed to speak volumes about acquaintances from church perhaps not being what they posed as.

Another friend, who grew up Mormon, assured me that she left the Mormon Church because all the Mormons she knew thought every other Mormon held direct conversations with God and believed they were the only ones who didn't.

And a therapist friend, an ex-pastor, said that unquestionably the most troubled people he dealt with were Christians.

One day all these comments came together and gave me an opinion about what could be done to cure the church of many of its ills. Somebody has to begin telling the truth about us, no matter how sordid. Because no person or institution can be healthy unless he, she, or it faces the honest to God, uncensored truth.

The question is, who's going to tell the truth?

Pastors aren't likely to, because too many truths are dangerous.

Which leaves the job for Christian artists, meaning all of us in general and writers in particular. We aren't dependent upon tithes and offerings, we don't need to worry about standing in front of a crowd and confessing, unless we choose to, and we can legitimately present the truth in a fictional package, where perhaps the only lie will be on the front-page, in the line that states "no characters or events are based on persons living or dead."

Believe This: God = Quality

Robert Pirsig's *Zen and the Art of Motorcycle Maintenance* is a treatise on attitude.

When I first read the book, I was home in San Diego for Christmas break from graduate studies at the University of Iowa Writers' Workshop. Laura, my first wife, myself, and our newborn Darcy had driven from San Diego to Iowa in August and returned in December in a Ford delivery van. It was the stripped-down model, with no insulation, a lack I had vowed to remedy before the return drive to a place that has winter.

My original plan was to line the walls inside with insulation and cover it with cardboard. But while reading *Zen and the Art*, which taught dedication to care and quality in all efforts, I couldn't let myself get away with that plan. So I bought a pile of redwood bender board and spent a whole week on the project. As long as I kept the van, looking at what I had done uplifted me.

Whether our current task is raising kids or counseling friends or writing stories or poems, we owe it to ourselves, families, friends, readers, and God, to use our gifts with care and dedication.

If we writers don't frequently ask ourselves "Can I do better?" and labor over every clumsy word; if we don't give our hearts to our stories and ask ourselves at least once on every page, "Am I being honest or just recycling clichés?" If we're not willing to revise until our brains reel from the effort, we'll be hacks.

The world doesn't need anymore hacks.

Way back when Ron Martina and I were roommates, he would look around at the clutter that had accumulated and pronounce, "Tons and tons of junk."

The same pronouncement could apply to many bookstores.

Do It As Unto the Lord

Olga Savitsky taught me (by example, as lessons are most profitably taught) why David was "a man after God's own heart."

I used to believe David earned that reputation because of his creative side, that God's heart was reflected in the David who wrote psalms. But Olga taught me about David's warrior side.

After she got diagnosed with cancer, Olga became an avid fan of "ultimate fighting," mixed martial arts, which at first troubled me. My son Cody had taken up the sport, and though I had learned plenty through Tae Kwon Do, the idea of professionals brutalizing each other for the amusement of spectators bothers me. I don't enjoy watching anyone get beaten, and the last person I'd ever want to see hit, or kicked, or thrown down and wrenched into submission, is my son. The second one I'd least want to see treated that way is anybody Cody might do it to. So, I failed to appreciate anybody for encouraging my son in that sport.

Meanwhile, Olga came to love mixed martial arts because it was as close to real fighting as our civilization allowed, with few restrictions except eye-gouging and murder. The fighters, she told me, go at it with every fiber of their bodies, nerves and wills, which gave her examples to follow in her fight against cancer.

Like David, Olga was a poet and a warrior, who during the battle devoted her all to believing; to studying scripture and applying its promises; to praying and meeting with the friends who lifted her spirit; and to avoiding those who weakened her, though she might love them. Sentenced to death, she devoted herself to the art of staying alive. To her, ultimate fighting was a perfect metaphor for the way God wants us to fight for all good (true, loving, and beautiful) things.

Which led me to better understand King David.

Before Olga, I tended to view the Old and New Testaments as separate books, since much of the Old Testament is stories and prophecies concerning strife and war, and the chief themes of the New Testament are love, redemption, and the peace they bring.

Olga made the books into one by teaching me that we can live in peace while at war. The better we love, the more peace we find. And to love better, we need to battle the powers of heaven and earth that create discord, destruction and all evils that use hypocrisy and lies in the effort to haunt, confuse, and embitter us.

To seek truth, as artists are called to do, is to battle against lies.

My grandma was Mary Garfield, a poet, storyteller and painter who insisted that lying was the behavior that grieved her most deeply. And I've come to feel the same. Among other evils, lies can lead even people of good will to perform cruel and barbaric acts.

While Olga helped me to understand Cody better and to admire him more (though I continue to hope he'll switch to a gentler sport), she taught me that King David was a man after God's own heart because he, like Olga, was both a warrior and a poet.

A warrior-poet.

The task of most warriors is to battle human enemies. The task of a warrior-poet is to battle lies, which are far more evil and treacherous than the most wicked humans.

Practice Patience

Master Jeong taught: "Number one is patience, number two is patience, number three is patience."

Deadlines help some of us. They make us get up and work. They offer us the vision of some respite from the pressure once we meet the deadline. They teach us discipline, something we can't be writers without.

But when deadlines rule us, we can lose our way. What should rule our writing lives is a pursuit of quality that persuades us to relegate deadlines to their proper place, as tools.

Unless we're salaried journalists, as writers we will either be the imposers of our deadlines or else we'll agree to them. Friends of mine who have become commercial successes with popular fiction are urged by their publishers to bring out at the very least a new book every year. The implied threat is that if they fail to do so, their bank accounts will suffer.

From the *New York Times*; "The e-book age has accelerated the metabolism of book publishing. Authors are now pulling the literary equivalent of a double-shift, churning out short stories, novellas or even an extra full-length book each year.

"They are trying to satisfy impatient readers who have become used to downloading any e-book they want at the touch of a button, and the publishers who are nudging them toward greater productivity in the belief that the more the authors' names are out in public, the bigger stars they will become.

"It used to be that once a year was a big deal," said Lisa Scottoline, a best selling author. 'You could saturate the market. But today the culture is a big hungry maw, and you have to feed it."

Even prior to the e-book age, many writers of romance, western, adventure and crime novels completed and published a dozen books a year. These folks might tell you that they need to produce like that to make a living. In the words of Ms. Scottoline, they are feeding our culture's big hungry maw.

I'll suggest that whether or not we choose to feed that creature might depend upon what realm we choose to live in, the world of popular commerce and culture, or the kingdom Christ called us to turn our allegiance to.

And I'll suggest that we can write millions of words and never leave behind anything memorable. Or, we might only write a few poems, short stories, articles, or song lyrics, yet change the lives of many, either directly or because our effect on a few readers helped them to write, or speak, or do great things.

The month I graduated from high school, I read a line that so affected me, I carried it on a note in my wallet until the note fell apart, then I wrote it again and carried that one. The line, from Dostoyevski's *Crime and*

Punishment, occurred when a father told of a dream that concerned how God would respond to his daughter Sonia, a humble girl driven to prostitution by the need to support her younger brothers and sisters. In the dream, God tells Sonia, "Your sins which are many are forgiven, for you have loved much."

A writer who chooses to make a living by consistently working on deadlines for dubious motives had better hope God grants him the same mercy he granted Sonia, "For by your words you will be justified, and by your words you will be condemned." Matthew 12:37

Those more concerned with speed than with quality are making product, not art. Maybe the Spirit will in some instances inspire such products. But as a rule, art requires patience, not deadlines.

Andre Dubus, author of many inspired short stories, tells of a method he calls writing vertically: "One day I decided to try a different approach. I told myself that I would not leave a sentence until I knew precisely what Anna (the story's main character) was feeling. For years, I had been writing horizontally, trying to move forward; now I would try to move down, as deeply as I could."

We can't expect a spirit to reveal much in an instant. To hear God, we usually need to quiet our rampaging minds and senses and listen.

If it takes an hour of sitting and waiting to find the

right image, to make a scene come alive or to deepen the truths it reveals, any artist will agree that was an hour valuably spent.

Albert Einstein once said, "It's not that I'm so smart. It's just that I stay with problems longer."

Repeat after me: "Number one is patience, number two is patience, number three is patience."

Get Perfect?

Somebody asked a master painter how to paint a perfect painting. He answered, "To paint a perfect painting, first become perfect, then paint."

So, I translated, to write a perfect story, become perfect then write.

I labored over this advice, judging how far from perfect I was, and wondering how far from perfect one could be and still create a masterpiece. And I considered that what I know about certain writers of masterpieces makes me believe they were not much more perfect in a human or spiritual sense than I am.

I decided the advice made no sense unless we interpret it this way: It's not essential to our writing that we be perfect, or even close, all the time, only when we're writing.

When we sit down (or stand up, or pace around) to write, we need to cast off imperfections such as our tendency to rush to judgment, our impatience, our preconceptions, our worries about whether we're going to succeed.

We need to clear our minds of anything that keeps us thinking or feeling out of accord with the fruits of the Spirit as described by Saint Paul, and try to approach our stories from an attitude of love, joy, peace, patience, kindness, goodness, faithfulness, gentleness and self-control.

Then we can treat our creations with deep respect and compassion. Even if we don't approach perfection for a nanosecond (most of us probably won't) the closer we come, the closer our creations may come to realizing their possibilities.

And the process of writing (or gardening, or fiddling) will be a spiritual exercise that draws us closer to what God would have us become.

Do Your Best

A student asked what she needed to do to get 100% on an assignment. I replied, "I don't know. I haven't ever given one." For quite a few years, I practiced Tae Kwon Do. The master was an international judge and a military academy instructor. He was ninth degree. In traditional Tae Kwon Do, nobody, repeat nobody, became tenth degree, because that would indicate perfection, with no room for improvement. I might give Feodor Dostoyevski a 99% for certain chapters of *Crime and Punishment* or *The Brothers Karamazov*. Maybe.

Another student told me that the instructor in a beginning Creative Writing class had remarked, "If you get an A, you can be a successful writer. Get a B, you might have a chance, but it's not likely. Get a C, forget it."

Unless this fellow gave everyone A's, that was not only a heartless remark, it was also patently false. I've known plenty of student writers who weren't in the least impressive but who have, through patience and dedication, become masterful.

Grades are perhaps a necessary evil of education. Evil because: behind every grade lies the question, "Compared to what?"

According to traditional Tae Kwon Do, our quest should not be for perfection, but to achieve a patient and indomitable spirit, and to always do our best.

Master Jeong made that advice into a chant, "Do your best. Do your best."

Go Home

Pointing to some children, Jesus said, "the kingdom of heaven belongs to such as these."

Which implies we can't be perfect unless we can be like children.

Since we all have been children, we're able to take real or imaginary journeys back to the places of our childhood, and to the people and dreams of that part of our lives. And once we get there, we can let those places, people and dreams refresh our minds and help us cast off jaded parts of ourselves, and go to the territory on the boundary of the kingdom of heaven where the Spirit most often seems to reside.

When I married and started a family I became someone other than who I am. I became somebody I'll call "Responsible Man". My grown children and their mother might argue, "You weren't all that responsible." But, though I did quit jobs and spend savings on the opportunity to write, we always had a home and food. My income always supported us. We never had to shop in thrift stores, except for furniture.

*

Master Jeong had us students sit in meditative posture. "Think about who you are," he said. "Not what you do. Think about who you are at your essence."

We are not who we generally feel or believe we are. What we feel we are is what we've become. Who we really are is closer to who we were as children.

Therapists sometimes guide people to seek their inner child. New Age gurus take men out into the woods and have them yowl and wield big sticks.

I told myself to banish "Responsible Man." I thought I could accomplish that, now that I owned a home in California and my big kids were grown and educated and had real jobs, and my little Zoë had a professional mama and income from me that she'll get no matter if I land in eternity or in some asylum. But "Responsible Man" wouldn't let go. He has become a parasite. Maybe he's my evil twin. Or maybe he knows that without him I'll go wild and wreak havoc upon the world. "Okay then," I tell him, "at least go to sleep when I'm writing."

The book *Born to Run* tells about a fellow people called *Caballo Blanco*, White Horse. He lived to run long races through wilderness. To achieve that life, he forsook most of the stuff that keeps the rest of us bound to place and routine. Us artists could learn from *Caballo Blanco*, who apparently discovered himself and lived accordingly.

At least we ought to learn how to put what we have become asleep long enough every day to let us find who we essentially are. So we can, either suddenly or gradually, learn how to be like the children Jesus pointed to when he proposed that to enter his kingdom we needed to become like them.

Behold The Secret of Art

During our wild youth, my friend Laurent obtained seaman's papers and found himself on the Mystic Mariner, bound for India. A fellow sailor supplied him with a psychedelic concoction, which resulted in Laurent standing all night on the bridge feeling certain that a space ship would soon come fetch him. The space aliens, he believed, would take him on a journey to planet where they would teach him the secret of art. Then they would deliver him back to earth.

Some years later, in church, Olga said she believed that when people prayed for her, the prayers were effective because the people who prayed loved her. A light flashed in my dim brain and I saw that prayers given in love will always be the ones most acceptable to God.

Because God is love, God exists in a dimension of love, and for us to communicate in that dimension, we have to enter that dimension and speak in that dimension's language.

Similarly, the more able we are to approach our writing with an attitude of love, the closer we will be to the dimension where the spirit that moves us resides, and the better we'll be able to translate its message.

In the book of Matthew, Christ commands us to

"Love your enemies, bless them that curse you, do good to them that hate you, and pray for them that spitefully use you and persecute you." He explains that if we only love our friends and do good to those who treat us well, we are no better than the worst of humanity.

The more and better we love, the closer we'll get to being like God, the master creator.

This then is the secret of art, about which space aliens failed to enlighten Laurent: to grow in our capacity to love, and to exercise that capacity.

In light of the above and Saint John's injunction that "perfect love casts out fear," let's suppose the Beatles were right in singing "Love is All You Need." Then let's exhort ourselves to love even the antagonists of our lives and our stories. And let's allow the power of that love to help us create fearlessly, without worrying about the judgment of readers, editors, reviewers, or the folks who sit next to us in church.

With our hearts and minds lightened by love and the absence of fear, the Spirit can easily move us.

Love One And All

Whenever a sermon, lecture or anybody tells me to change a habit or attitude but doesn't attempt to clue me how to do so, I get either petulant or skeptical or both. So I can hardly suggest we should love better then drop the subject.

Since way back, I have been a devotee of books, articles, and scriptures about love. And, in addition to the Bible, the book I most often recommend is SØren Kiekegaard's *Works of Love.*

Kierkegaard compels us to learn to read differently. He won't allow us to skim, or to overlook the depth of loaded words.

Most of us read Scripture in the W.C. Fields manner.

Someone encountered Fields, a master comedian, on his deathbed reading a Bible. When the person asked if he had gotten religion, Fields replied, "I'm looking for a loophole."

Kierkegaard uses a different approach. When he writes about Christ, he not only takes Christ's words at face value, he takes them to heart and applies them to reality no matter how severely they may insult or outrage.

Works of Love is essentially a treatise on Matthew 22:39: "... You shall love your neighbor as yourself."

The book's premise is, when Christ commands us to love our neighbor as ourselves, he is commanding us to "love without distinction."

Note that verse reads, we "shall", not "should," love our neighbor. A command, not a suggestion.

As the parable of "The Good Samaritan" clarifies, our neighbor is whomever we encounter in need. Since all human beings are in need of something, that's quite a chore, which Kierkegaard translates to mean we are commanded to love everybody, without distinction.

If a parent stops to ponder the command and asks how does it apply to the art of parenting, he might discover the will to love the neighbor kid he previously thought of as simply a pest and danger to his daughter.

Or a writer might discover that she is called to devote attention to all her characters and bring them to life.

Love Like Whitman

"Love the earth and sun and animals. Despise riches, give alms to everyone that asks. Stand up for the stupid and crazy. Devote your income and labor to others... And your very flesh shall be a great poem."
Walt Whitman

Love Your Characters

I told my daughter Darcy I'd been convicted to take more seriously the injunction to love our enemies.

"But suppose," I said, "a neighbor comes roaring home daily at three a.m. in his nineteen-fifty-five Chevy with dual glass-pack mufflers. And suppose when I ask him to quit roaring he only says, 'You think I should walk?' Then he laughs and slams his door on me.

"Now, my question is, what does it mean to love him? If I act like his friend, he might interpret that attitude as approval of his behavior."

Darcy said she believes loving your enemy means doing your best to understand him by considering the things that might've caused him to act like a jerk. An ethicist or theologian might call that interpretation of love overly simple. Still, it's useful. Most often, if we can understand what fears and insecurities could lead somebody to offend us, we'll let go of a grudge and be healthier for it, and not act rashly against the person.

We can apply this sort of love to our characters. Read any Dickens novel and you'll notice that, with few exceptions, the author appears to have a deep sympathy for all his characters. He relishes their uniqueness and does his best to present their quirks and motives in ways that make them come alive and that remind us to beware of passing judgment.

Love Your Work

Flannery O'Connor was one of the great originals. She could be honest, profound and outrageous all at once. So I value her opinion more than most people's.

In *Mystery and Manners*, a book of her essays, she proposes, "If writing is your vocation, then, as a writer, you will seek the will of God first through the laws and limitations of what you are creating; your first concern will be the necessities that present themselves in the work."

O'Connor explains, "If the writer's attention is on producing a work of art, he is going to take great pains to control every excess, everything that does not contribute to this central meaning and design. He cannot indulge in sentimentality, in propagandizing, or in pornography and create a work of art, for all these things are excesses. They call attention to themselves and distract from the work as a whole."

At first, this appears to contradict a contention of Fredrick Buechner's that *The Brothers* Karamazov is, "a book which, just because Dostoyevsky leaves room in it for whatever comes up to enter, is entered here and there by maybe nothing less than the Holy Spirit."

So which are we to trust, O'Connor's aesthetics or Dostoyevski's?

O'Connor contented that writers ought to push their talents to the outermost limit of the kind of talent they have. If we presented her with Buechner's assessment, I can imagine her reminding us that we're not Dostoyevski. He had his limits, we have ours, and a crucial part of our task is to define them.

Modern writers, she argues, "are not content to stay within our limitations and make something that is simply a good in and by itself.... Yet what is good in itself glorifies God because it reflects God."

Because it is both true and beautiful.

We need to love our work for its own sake, to take it to the outer limits of our current talent and ability, but not beyond, unless taken beyond by the spirit that moves us.

And we need to disallow the temptation to use our stories as vehicles for preaching or propagandizing except insofar as the stories themselves call us to.

"The artist has his hands full and does his duty if he attends to his art," O'Connor maintains. "He can safely leave evangelizing to the evangelists." She would have us Christians realize that Christian stories are not necessarily about Christians and their concerns but are simply fiction "in which the truth as Christians know it has been used as a light to see the world by."

Consider Your Motive

A story I read to an audience at California State University, San Marcos included a scene from a long ago Billy Graham crusade. After the story, during question time, a student asked me if I had an agenda for my work.

In my rambling way, I explained that with each piece, I might have the different agenda, which is promoting my view of the world in the context of the given story. But the only overall agenda I'm conscious of is to suggest to people that they seek the truth with an open heart and open mind.

Some of my work might appear to promote Christian beliefs but that truly is not my intention. I only would hope readers might choose to look into Christian beliefs and reconsider their attitudes toward them. And that would apply to people who already believe as well as people who don't. Once we think we have the truth and don't need to seek it any longer, we're dangerous.

Each year Pastor Ed Noble of Journey Church gives a series called "God at the Movies."

While introducing the series, he commented that lots of believers limit their watching and reading of stories to the stuff "Christian" authors and producers offer, which is usually an attempt to adapt the kind of "secular" art they appreciate into stories the most delicate believers won't find offensive.

So, these readers and viewers partake in largely derivative stories with all but the least dangerous truths bleached out of them.

Better, he suggested, to realize that God appears in stories no matter the author's beliefs or intentions. Better for us to read secular stories with an eye for spiritual truth than to waste our time on stories that will only reinforce our safe beliefs.

And I'll add, better for artists of Christian beliefs to give up pandering and approach their work with an attitude like Flannery O'Connor's when she advised that Christian fiction is simply honest fiction written by a Christian.

Note in particular the word *honest*.

I guess I'm writing in an effort to learn and express the truth because my best happiness lies in discovery and in sharing what I learn with other people.

What's your motive?

Let God Be the Judge

When I wrote feature articles for the *San Diego Reader,* I was blessed with a truly fine editor, Judith Moore.

I was attending Faith Chapel, where a man got accused of molesting kids in the nursery. During his trial, the church became a laughingstock, because children were testifying to outrageous stuff such as this man had taken them in a bus to a zoo and sacrificed elephants.

Local talk shows held the church up as a place where nut jobs skulked around hunting for demons in the closets. But I hadn't found anymore nut jobs at church than anywhere else. So I pitched an article to Judith.

While writing and researching, I got incensed about the talk shows' and trial defense team's portrayal of the church, and about therapists who apparently had little idea how to lure the truth, rather than wild imaginings, out of children.

I worked on the article for many days but couldn't get it right. Judith called and asked how it was coming. When I told her, she said, "Send it." I did, and soon she called again. She said, "Ken, you don't do anger. You don't condemn people."

After that, the article was a pleasure to write, and I have always felt good about it.

And I learned two crucial lessons.

One: If a story isn't working, we ought to ask, could the spirit have set up a blockade? Could we be trying to write something that isn't us?

Two: When Christ was on earth, as far as we know, the only people who seemed to rouse his anger were hypocrites. And Christ could recognize hypocrisy, but I can't. To know for certain if someone is a hypocrite, I would need to see inside his mind and heart. Christ could do that. I can't.

Saint James warned us, "Judgment will be merciless to him who has shown no mercy; mercy triumphs over judgment."

We weren't put on earth to judge one another.

What I learned from that story about the danger of passing judgments rendered me less adamant or certain about the judgments I make, and prepared me to discover the theme of the my novel *The Good Know Nothing*.

As writers we're obliged to judge in the sense of recognizing the errors our characters make and holding them accountable. But if we approach our stories with an attitude as free of judgment as we can make it, our bad guys won't be just bad guys. They'll be bad guys because ____, or bad guys, but ____. (Fill in the blanks.)

Stalk the Truth

During the months after the Faith Chapel article appeared in the *San Diego Reader*, dozens of people told me the article helped them and their families to heal.

If we try our best to write truth, and approach the task humbly, we have every right to believe the truth will be revealed. And if we write the truth, it will make things happen.

I had come to Faith Chapel because I felt God urging me to find a church and use it at least as a place to give thanks for a life that felt blessed.

My cousin Patti attended Faith Chapel. She had lured me there for Christmas productions. The place and its people had impressed me as rather slick and superficial. But when I showed up one Sunday, I discovered Pastor Charlie.

His father, George Gregg, had overseen the growth of Faith Chapel from a small gathering to a membership of thousands. During the 1960s, the church became famous around San Diego for welcoming everybody, even hippies.

But Charlie was the one who kept me coming back. I got drawn by his quiet sincerity and his messages that illuminated text better than any professor I had studied under.

Then Charlie left the church. And George Gregg died suddenly. When my article came out, the Gregg family was enduring hard times, in part on account of the trial and the shadow it cast over their church, which was George's legacy.

Not long after the article appeared, I received a note from Charlie. He thanked me for the story and claimed it had helped his family heal.

If that article was my only creation, I could feel justified in becoming a writer, as the effort had blessed somebody.

Lie in Search of the Truth?

The truth we stalk may be involved with actual people and real happenings, but we may well find the best route to truth is by way of fictional characters and events.

George Garrett edited a collection of short stories and called it *The Liar's Craft*. Fiction may be composed of lies, but that doesn't keep it from revealing truth. Because truth is found in the meanings, the connections, the deep currents of stories. Sticking to verifiable details may stop us from tunneling into the depths where our imaginations, and the Spirit, would otherwise lead us.

In fiction, we have a license to lie at will. Non-fiction stories impose limits, as was most evident in the fuss over James Frey's fabrications in *A Million Little Pieces*.

In non-fiction, our ability to simplify, embellish, guess or otherwise distort the facts as we know them should be set by our intentions.

To the extent that we're dedicated to seeking and writing truth, we can alter perceived fact, say for the purpose of achieving dramatic unity or to render a character more understandable than he or she might be from the factual rendition of a certain incident. But to the extent that we mean to deceive, aggrandize ourselves, or gain rewards at the expense of truth, we deserve derision and punishment.

Get Free

Everybody wants to be free, right?

We read that the truth will set us free.

We're told Christ came to free us, and that if he sets us free, we are free indeed.

One of the liberties we in the U.S. at least claim to prize is the freedom to speak the truth as we see it. Yet we allow dogmas, editors, critical readers, and the marketplace, to censor us.

The Brothers Karamazov addresses the concept of freedom. In the "Grand Inquisitor" chapter, Dostoyevski sets up a drama in which Christ returns to earth in medieval Europe, gets taken captive by the Inquisition and told by the Inquisitor why he failed: because people don't really want the freedom he granted.

What people want, the Inquisitor contends, is what Satan, while tempting Christ at the end of his forty-day fast in the desert, offered to help Christ provide them:

Miracle. A show so grand it would stop all questioning.

Mystery. Idols to worship.

Authority. A source of unambiguous, strict rules that everybody must follow, so they won't feel lost, alone or different.

As writers, we can't afford to be like the people

Satan (in the Inquisitor's story) describes.

If we hope to leave ourselves open to the spirit that moves us, we need to question everything, beware of idols such as the desire for fame and wealth, and to express our uniqueness.

If we're Christian writers, redemption can free us from the demons of guilt and shame. If this freedom allows us to shed legalistic inhibitions, fear of risking heresy, and whatever hang-ups are blocking the messages the spirit is ready to give us, I suspect we can create more powerful art than writers who haven't found the ticket to freedom.

Practice Freedom

Churches take the position that freedom is found in submission to their commandments, doctrines and hierarchies. Though I'm convinced there's more to the freedom Christ offers than submission alone can grant, the churches' position exposes a truth we writers can learn from.

Dashiell Hammett, in an unfinished novel called *Tulip*, maintains that everybody has good stories, but they're only worth writing or reading once they've been given an effective structure.

More than any other factor, structures are what make our stories, our essays, our dance routines, or sporting events compelling.

Structure frees us writers from the fear or anxiety of having to be a great stylist, as even a mediocre stylist can entertain readers as long as she's working with a solid structure.

Structure can free us from the nagging doubt that our story will find a right ending.

Structure may serve as the place where beauty and truth will come to dwell. In *Summa Theologica*, St. Thomas Aquinas wrote, "Beauty and goodness in a thing are identical fundamentally; for they are based upon the same thing, namely, the form; and consequently goodness is praised as beauty."

Pursue Beauty

Rainer Maria Rilke argues in "The First Elegy":
"For beauty is nothing but the beginning of terror, which we are just able to endure, and we are so awed because it serenely disdains to annihilate us. Every angel is terrifying."

When Søren Kierkegaard defines "dread" as the apprehension of the possibilities freedom offers, I believe he tells us why, as Rilke contends, every angel is terrifying. To Kierkegaard, "This dread is the dizziness of freedom which occurs when the spirit would posit the synthesis [the uniting of body and soul], and gazes down into its own possibility, grasping at finiteness to sustain itself."

Angels terrify us and the dizziness of dread makes us flee from them, because they are reflections of God. The Old Testament holds that if we saw God we would surely die. Because God is more beautiful than he created us to bear. So he gave Christ, his appearance moderated by his humanity, as our standard of truth and beauty.

Yet beauty doesn't only reside in the divine and the good. Beauty also resides in great sinners, in horror, death, all kinds of darkness, wonder, and tragedy.

Pleasant is no synonym for beautiful. Remember

the words of John Keats: "Beauty is truth, truth beauty. That is all we know on earth and all we need to know."

The best synonym for beautiful is true.

Beauty resides in the heights and the depths, in all the places we dizzy writers are sometimes obliged to go, if we hope to write the truth.

Get Enthused

Branch Rickey (1881–1965) was a baseball executive best remembered for: breaking Major League Baseball's color barrier by signing Jackie Robinson and drafting Roberto Clemente; creating the framework for the modern minor league system; and introducing the batting helmet. His achievements and outspoken Christian faith earned him the nickname 'the Mahātmā.'"

This wise and accomplished fellow advised, "Prefer excesses of enthusiasm to the complacency of wisdom."

Which doesn't work as a sound bite, as it's easily misinterpreted to mean prefer enthusiasm to wisdom.

To me, it means, when wisdom becomes complacent, it threatens to nullify the enthusiasm that arises from passion, imagination, or inspiration.

In the context of writing, the proper role of wisdom (craft) is to serve enthusiasm (art).

For instance, wisdom ought to remind us that not every passage delivered from a passionate or inspired heart is a gem to be shared with readers. Some of them will only speak to us, or only make sense to us if we are in a certain frame of mind. And even the real gems might not deserve to be in the context we've placed them, if they intrude upon the story.

All of which is why some folks claim writing can't be taught and some claim it can. Craft can be readily learned. Passion, imagination, and the openness to inspiration, not so readily.

Pay Your Dues, Part One

After his victory over the tempter in the wilderness, Jesus returned in the "power of the Spirit." In other words, Christ had to face temptation before the full power of the Spirit was available to him.

Likewise, we may need to prove ourselves ready for the gifts of inspiration.

At the University of Iowa, at a party after a reading, I was talking to Sara Vogan and C. E. Poverman (alias Buzz). Sara was my friend and fellow student. Buzz had come to give the reading. Sara asked Buzz, who had finished Iowa's writers' workshop program a few years before, how long it usually took graduates before they sold a book. Buzz replied that even the writers who succeed most always take ten years from the time they got serious about writing.

He was dead right, I've observed. And who can count the ones who fail or drop out along the way?

I began to write in earnest soon after I realized my dad, not I, was the musician in our family, and I was the storyteller.

By "in earnest" I mean every chance I could. If the workdays burnt me out, I would write all weekend. If kids demanded my weekends, I rose early and wrote.

I hauled a wife and baby to Iowa largely because I

imagined earning a graduate degree that qualified me to teach writing at a college would allow me more time to write than most professions would.

I don't mean to whine. If anybody sacrificed because of my choices, it was my family, not me. My life has been a great adventure.

What I do mean is this:

If you want the Spirit's help with your writing, the Spirit may require that you make writing one of your top priorities.

I heard about a South Korean man who instantly became a hero of mine. Having been imprisoned in a North Korean labor camp for some political crime, he and another former prisoner wrote and were producing an operatic musical about those camps. They found potential backers, but the South Korean government pressured the backers to withdraw and thereby avoid public outcry that could damage economic cooperation with North Korea.

So this producer mortgaged his kidney to pay for the production.

Let's think about him when we lament missing Saturday morning volleyball in favor of writing.

Pay Your Dues, Part Two

An element of what we'd call a talent or gift is the ability or the will to do whatever is required to develop it.

When people say, as many do, to be a writer you need to write every day, what they actually mean is, you need to be willing and able to spend whatever time and energy is required to transform your potential gift or talent into a flourishing one.

I took up guitar when I was twelve. But I never could make myself spend more than about ten minutes a day actually practicing. I might play longer, but not work on scales or on learning new and difficult riffs. Many years later, I'm no better at guitar than I was at fourteen. But even now, I could gain some real mastery if I would force myself to practice a half hour a day.

My dad built and operated a par three golf course. Most of my life, I've played golf, but I'll never be able to approach par regularly unless I play at least a couple times a week and add to that several hours on the driving range and another few hours chipping and putting.

The point is, I could be a good (though probably not great) musician or a superior golfer if I would, and could make myself, put in the required time and energy.

We're born with gifts. Making them work or not is our choice.

Pay Your Dues, Part Three

I have a problem with ways some churches promote the principle of tithing. But the principle of giving our resources in thanks for what we are given (by God, an institution, a business, or a person) makes perfect sense.

Master Jeong didn't abide deadbeats. Without ranting or preaching, he made clear to us that the first responsibility of a martial artist is to honor the people he learns from.

Let's ask why God should bless us with inspiration if we don't make a priority of blessing those who teach or help us.

If we take a class, let's pay for it. Even if it's virtually free, say at a community college or a church, let's do the courtesy of asking the instructor if she has a book, and if she does, let's buy it.

Let's not be the people who go to a reading or a book signing and approach the author with no intention of buying her book, but only to ask questions we hope can further our writing careers.

I will restrain my wicked urge to give examples.

Banish Ambition

Raymond Carver, master of the short story, advised us to write every day without anxiety or ambition.

He claimed his stories reached a higher level when he began to follow that advice.

Ambition may drive us to work harder, but unless we can leave it outside when we go to our writing places, it shifts our attention out of the present, makes us strive to please. Worse, it may spark the temptation to imitate, and while we're imitating, we're not being ourselves. Being ourselves, expressing our unique angle on life in our unique voice, has to be our goal.

Worst of all, ambition distances us from our imaginations and from the spirit that moves us.

Ambition, like perfectionism, is a killer.

Be Justified

Here's a letter a friend sent me after I had helped him through the process of writing and revising his strange and poignant life story:

"Dear Ken, a non-Christian friend who is quite literate and who has read a portion of my manuscript suggested that I e-mail [a certain agent who had expressed interest] to follow up. My friend was pretty negative regarding the Christian stuff and felt [the agent] would flat out reject working with it. She suggested I tell him that, in essence, I am aware the book has a slant that might not appeal to many publishers, therefore I would be glad to do further work so it is spiritual, but not so evangelical. What do you think? Do you think I should follow up in any way or wait to hear back from [the agent]. I sent him the manuscript a week ago. Of course the purpose of the book is to testify of God's work in my life and in the lives of others. The idea of altering the book too much doesn't set well with me."

Here's part of my reply:

"Prosperity gospels aside, I'd bet God would rather have us write the truth than write a bestseller. Pardon my preaching, but your friend's comments made me crazy."

In *The Measure of Maturity* Francis Frangipane writes, "God judges the quality of our entire lives by the soundness and substance of our words. Thus Jesus warned, 'But I tell you that every careless word that people speak, they shall give an accounting for it in the day of judgment. For by your words you will be justified, and by your words you will be condemned.'"

four — Assignments etc.

Get Humble

I have known lots of writers, some of whom I have watched grow from novices to masters. And I've observed that the masters and the ones I suspect are on their way to that level have in common their desire to learn and their willingness to set ego aside to ask for help and listen.

A problem rises from the nature of most artists: we need to be hypersensitive, and vulnerable to emotions, in order to give our art passion and to make a way for the Spirit to reach us. We also need to be bold, unwilling to run from experience or pain that can give us insights to pass along. So we can't take the easy route to boldness, which is denial of fear and other troubling emotions.

When I observe a beginning writer who appears terrified to receive criticism yet asks for it, and who listens even while it batters his heart, I believe I've encountered a potentially fine writer.

One such person was a student at the University of Arizona when I taught there. Since he had finished the MFA in writing before I came, and had gone on to seek the PhD in literature, he didn't have the occasion to take any of my classes, yet he brought me stories to read and listened eagerly to my comments.

He was no great writer at the time. But he became a master and won the Pulitzer Prize in fiction.

On the other hand, I've known dozens of students, passionate writers amongst them, who respond to critiques with explanations and excuses. I can't think of any of them who have yet sold a book to a publisher.

Authors who publish and get acclaim often slip into thinking they have arrived, they have magic, their words are golden and they're beyond the point of worrying much about story structure, readers' expectations for a particular genre, or anything else that will restrain them.

They're usually quite wrong. I know I was.

Publishing a book, even to high praise, should make us more humble, more grateful to the spirit that moved us and the people who helped nudge us along. It should make us look closely for what we did right and use that knowledge to inform our next story while we also attempt to grow and reach for the next challenge.

Just because we can climb the first rung of a ladder doesn't mean we can fly.

Not long ago I gave a manuscript copy of a new novel to Dana Crowell, a student of mine, and asked for her comments.

She gave it back with lots of praise and this critique:

"My biggest issue was with sentence length. Some of the sentences were so long, I had to reread them several times to follow the story. Michael Seidman [an editor of popular mysteries] says that for commercial books, a sentence should be between 8-12 words long, a paragraph no more than 9 lines. Some of your sentences have 52 words. Just something to think about. The sentence length stopped me."

I wondered, did Faulkner have to put up with such trivia?

But that's no concern of mine. My concern, the question I need to ask: Does God want me (not Faulkner) to work with this advice?

I tend to push and perhaps delude myself with the notion that God would have me reach a wide audience, which is one reason I often write suspense and mystery.

So, after reading Dana's note, given what I had read and heard about the average reading level of popular fiction, and given that Dana got stopped by some of my sentences though she is quite literate, I chose to heed her comments.

But I didn't take them at face value. I took them under consideration and gave myself a task I hoped would better inform me on the sentence length issue. I picked up Michael Connelly's last book and read it with an eye to sentence length.

What I found humbled me. To find out why, read on.

Get Courageous

In a newspaper interview, a University of Iowa professor advised writers: if you have a boyfriend or girlfriend, get rid of them; if you've got a husband or wife, disown them; if you've got kids, drown them.

He must've been experiencing a troubled and ornery day.

No matter how vehemently I disapprove of his solution, at least the part about the children, I'll agree, along with Saint Paul, on the basic principle: lovers and dependents can get in the way of our work.

If you dedicate yourself to writing, at some point you'll suspect people are conspiring to stop you. They will demean your efforts overtly or by lack of appreciation. Your family will fail to hide their resentment of the time you spend dreaming over the keyboard and the fact that you don't make as much money as you could if you applied the same effort to pulling weeds for minimum wage.

And when you're having a creative reverie, or even if they catch you transcribing directly from the Spirit, they will interrupt.

We can't blame them. When pursuing our art, we're lost to the world. We're remote, boring, often cranky. We're loners who may elicit jealousy when our loved ones begin to doubt we really need them.

But most of us do need them, at least in times when we're not creating. So, if I were asked for advice on this issue, I might suggest we try hard to be extra good to our loved ones whenever we break away from our art.

The primary goal of most people is to feel loved. If, through word and action, we convince our families and friends we cherish them, they will most likely agree to leave us alone to our reveries.

Otherwise, we might try earplugs and a lock on the office door.

It's a given that in practicing art, we risk alienating family and friends. Even if we do our best for them, we may not be model husbands, wives or parents. But neither are soldiers, policemen or preachers, other occupations that require will and courage.

As Olga taught me, King David was "a man after God's own heart" because he was both a warrior and a poet. I imagine David composing his psalms with the same focus, zeal, and courage as he used attacking Goliath or the Edomites.

Quit Making Excuses

At least until you get six-figure advances, when you meet people and they ask what you do, beware of telling them you're a writer. Too often they'll think you make lots of money. If you're honest, you'll admit you don't. And suddenly they won't appear to find you as interesting as they did when they saw dollar signs.

Or they'll tell you they too are going to become writers as soon as they can find the time.

Nobody I've ever met has ample time to write. We get the time by stealing it. We take jobs that give us long weekends, and/or find part-time jobs or husbands or wives who won't expect much money out of us, and/or take our kids to day-care and hustle or pray for tuition money, and/or resign ourselves to five or six hours of sleep a night and/or pass up weekend softball leagues or vacations. When our family suggests a day trip to the beach, we often ask them to go without us and spend our first hour of freed writing time suffering flashbacks of their parting looks or comments.

One evening in Tae Kwon Do, when the time for my black belt test was nearing, I encountered Master Jeong in the locker room and explained why I wasn't coming to class often enough and admitted I realized that to progress required at least three classes a week. I meant to come more often, I told him, once Little League season ended and released me from managing Cody's baseball team.

Master Jeong listened to all that. Then, without a nod, a grimace or a word, he turned and walked off. I supposed he was preoccupied.

A week or so later, I found him in a congenial mood. We chatted about some mutual concerns before, once again, I explained my failure to attend more often.

Without expression or comment, he walked away.

After three or four such responses (I'm not always quick-witted), I recognized that people making excuses, reasonable or not, might as well be invisible, and inaudible.

Why we fail to perform doesn't matter. Our reasons are of no consequence. Missing classes (or writing sessions) because of working the three jobs I need to send my daughter to college will affect my performance in the same way as if I missed them because of an addiction to *Survivor*.

To earn a black belt, I needed to change my habits. Simple.

Be Indomitable

Master Jeong taught that the Tae Kwon Do spirit (probably not to be confused with the spirit that moves us) is an indomitable spirit.

Sometimes when your world has crashed, it's wise to tell yourself, "I have an indomitable spirit." Say it enough, you may believe it. Believe it, and it may come true.

I used to keep a file of rejection letters, thinking once they stopped coming, I would use the collection to wallpaper a room. That was before I realized they may never stop coming. I got one this morning.

Here's a grim fact of life. If you're not getting rejected by somebody for something, you've probably stopped dreaming, which may be the most dangerous thing an artist can do.

Rejections may come from friends. Suppose you spend a year writing a novel, you give a copy to a *compadre*, and learn a few weeks later that he has not only put off opening your book, but during that time he's bought and read two Dean Koontz thrillers. No matter what excuse he gives, your feelings get hurt.

In writers' groups, we judge the worth of our stories by every remark, sigh, modulation of voice and facial expression. If our feelings don't get hurt even a little, either we have achieved something like nirvana or become experts at the dubious skill of turning hurt to anger, which sooner or later will either kill us or send any bright spirit into exile.

Agents and editors sometimes reject us in brutal ways. I once submitted a baseball novel and after about four months received a note, "Sorry you struck out with us." Either this prominent editor hadn't gleaned that people who devote well over a year to a project don't consider their work a joke, or she had a mean streak the size of and a heart the temperature of Siberia.

I won't give her name but will note that she has recently surfaced as a panelist on a radio show called *Wait, Wait, Don't Tell Me.*

Suppose that after ten years of dedicated work you publish your first novel and feel you deserve at least a modicum of respect. You've gotten fine reviews. Then you pick up another review and think it must've been written by somebody who didn't read more than five pages of your novel and, moreover, mistook you for the guy who stole his wife.

Anyone who has suffered such a review, or had a nightmare about receiving one, should read Tobias Woolf's short story, "A Bullet in the Brain," in which a book reviewer who gets taken hostage by bank robbers criticizes his captors until the joyous ending, which I won't give away any more of than I already have.

In case I haven't made my point, it's this: as a

writer, you're going to get rejected. So you'd better protect yourself by learning how to cope with rejection.

Friedrich Nietzsche gave the simple answer to this problem. He wrote, "Creators are hard."

Okay, but the best creators are also soft. They're vulnerable, open to a deep and wide range of emotion. They're pliable, willing to ditch their most cherished preconceptions for new truths and inspirations.

So let's define "hard" as "resilient" rather than as "solid" or "dense". Let's be willing to stretch ourselves even to the breaking point by mustering confidence in our ability to repair our hearts or by trusting that God will repair us.

A few gimmicks have helped me recover from rejection. The simplest is realizing that no one person can determine how other readers will react. *Midheaven*, my first novel, went to three editors. The first reported that he liked the story but not the narrator. The second liked the narrator but not the story. The third liked both and bought the book.

On the surface, where we generally live, we can ease the pain of rejection by already having in mind a next book and being so excited about it we can convince ourselves no sane person could reject it.

As my friend writer Don Purviance once asked, "Are you in it for the long haul, or aren't you?"

Still, rejections can send me to wallow in self-doubt and agony until I persuade my heavy heart that my motive for writing isn't to become the darling of editors and critics.

At a deep level, wisdom suggests that our writing should be about giving love, not getting it.

Master Jeong asked us, "How do you be good teacher?" Students tossed out sensible but wrong answers until Master Jeong said, "Love your students."

In a real sense, our readers are our students. Our stories teach, whether or not we mean for them to.

Love can be defined as the willingness to sacrifice to promote the spiritual growth of another.

Writing ought to be a sacrifice of our time, passion and energy to create a gift of love.

Find Out Who You Are

According to the TV show *Joan of Arcadia,* which I recommend buying on DVD (for some insidious reason, it got cancelled), St Augustine wrote, "To know yourself is to know God."

Telling our stories is an adventure. We might know what has happened in our past, but as we write or tell it, new insights and meanings come clear. In the process of recalling and recounting our stories, we discover our lives.

As storytellers who draw on our experience, we see evidence that life isn't a random collection of events. Rather, it appears to move in accord with some larger plan that forces us to confront our fears and weaknesses. We remember strange happenings at crucial moments. Events we once saw as catastrophes now appear as blessings.

Our life stories may become a foundation of our faith. In his essay "Faith and Fiction," Frederick Buechner maintains that our faith has the same beginnings as our fiction, in "the awareness of events in our lives that lead from one to the other and thereby give each other meaning. The ups and downs of the years, the dreams, the odd moment, the intuitions."

The plots of our lives are foundations of our faith as

well as the germs and cornerstones of the stories we write. Never mind whether we call the stories fact or fiction.

Ask Who You Are

In Tucson, my second home and writing retreat, I wake up and walk a few blocks to Starbucks and think or make notes or whatever. Last summer, I would go there at about 5:30. Beginning on the walk, plenty of ideas would come. But in winter I found myself staying up later and awaking at first light, about 6:30, and finding that no or few ideas came. Then one morning I woke up at 5, worried about my little Zoë in San Diego, who had been sick for a few days. I walked to Starbucks at 5:30 and plenty of ideas came. So I made up my mind to go to sleep earlier, because 5:30 seems my best time for ideas. At least in Tucson.

If something works, go with it.

One desert evening, the DJ of a classical music station told about a Finnish composer who, because he needed to support himself and his family by farming, didn't compose much compared to the composers who were privileged and could concentrate on their music.

The next morning on the walk, about a half-mile, I thought about yesterday's excursion to Walmart. When I passed the book section, I noticed two large inspirational collections, one in English, one in Spanish. My dark side was stricken by envy. Since my adult life has been somewhat defined by the need to hold a day job while writing, as did the Finnish composer, the idea of shelf space in Walmart appeals to me.

Halfway to Starbuck's, I began searching for a catchy, general reader title that might fool corporate book buyers and Walmart shoppers into thinking my book's advice would apply not only to artists, but to all humanity. Which of course it does. But I could make that much clearer, slant the book more toward self-help or...

The Spirit stopped me, with a feeling I might translate as, "Who do you think you are?"

I asked out loud, "Okay, so who am I?"

"You're a guy who tries to write the truth," I heard. "Try to reach everybody, the effort will make you a liar."

As Spanky of the *Little Rascals* would say, "There you go."

Become Who You Are

To a question implied by the aforementioned article on ChristianityToday.com: Shouldn't we Christians be more inspired than other artists? I think we should.

Then, I wonder, are we?

I have read a fair sample of contemporary Christian books and come away discouraged because I haven't found much in the way of original insights or visions. So to the question, are we Christians more inspired than other artists, I would have to answer, I don't see evidence that we are.

Suppose I'm right. Then why *aren't* we Christians more inspired than other artists.

I'll suggest the answer might be that we write as adults, who have been robbed of our unique selves and programmed by the desire to succeed in the eyes of the world, whether by the world we mean the whole society, our Christian subculture, or the expectations of publishers.

Too often we write what we think we are supposed to write, to get us money, or acclaim, or whatever else we need or think we need. I've got no beef against writing for money. But when we are writing by strict prescription, we may not allow ourselves to be ourselves. As I mention before but will repeat as the truth often calls for repeating, Friedrich Nietzsche, who made a career out of rebelling against God, but who was a very smart fellow, famously advised people to "Become who you are."

I know a writer of contemporary mysteries with antecedents in history. Say, something happened during the Civil War that prompted a murder in 2012 Washington. When she writes the historical part, she is most engaging. But not so much with the contemporary part. Because she has in her mind that mysteries should be written in a certain style, but she has no such preconception about the historical stories. In other words, she is more herself when writing the historical parts.

We should be writing as the children God created us to be, the unique selves with the unique curiosities, unique visions, points of view, and on the unique quests we were created for.

In a series of messages entitled *Artisan*, Erwin McManus, of Mosaic Church, quotes Pablo Picasso as saying that all children are artists, but very few adults are.

Matthew 18:3; "Truly I say to you, unless you are converted and *become like children*, you will not enter the kingdom of heaven."

I've often wondered, what *exactly* does that mean?

Raymond Carver, one of the best short story writers ever, commented, "Writers don't need tricks or gimmicks or even necessarily need to be the smartest fellows on the block. At the risk of appearing foolish, a writer sometimes needs to be able to just stand and gape at this or that thing--a sunset or an old shoe--in absolute and simple amazement."

Like children can.

Notice in Matthew 18:3 Christ uses the verb "become". Become like children. To enter the kingdom of heaven we need to be reborn as the children we were. As ourselves. Only with the wisdom to set aside the selfish parts of our natures.

The place to begin making our writing engaging and vital is to write as ourselves. We need to get de-programmed.

Remember Who You Are

When Zoë was seven, she asked who would be fighting in the war at the end of the world.

Pam said, "Probably Arabs and Israelis."

"Which ones are the good guys?" Zoë asked.

After a moment of reflection, I said, "I suspect there'll be good guys on both sides."

"Okay," she said. "But who should we vote for?"

Now, I'm all for a bit of childhood indoctrination, but to ask a seven-year-old to take sides against anybody feels wrong, as my strongest desire as a parent is to help my kids hold on to their innocence as long as they can without endangering themselves. So, I sighed relief when she said, "If Texas was one of the teams, we would vote for them, wouldn't we?"

"Well," I said, "Who would the other team be?"

"Los Angeles. So we should vote for Los Angeles, right?"

How I love that girl.

While I was writing *The Biggest Liar in Los Angeles*, which is set in the 1920s, Zoë and I watched *Chinatown*. Not set in the '20s, but close enough. Of course I had to send my little girl out of the room a few times, and get creative with certain explanations.

Zoë's questions and observations entertained me

nearly as much as the movie did.

When, during a drought, Jake the detective follows Hollis Mulwray to the coast and sits on a rocky cliff watching while Mulwray observes water pour out of the storm drains, Zoë got scared for Jake because she saw a dinosaur hiding in the rocks. Which puts a great film into a whole new light.

We have a flexible one-hour a day time limit on television watching. Zoë asked if movies counted the same as TV shows. I said if it's a good movie, longer is okay. I remarked that a half-hour of Sponge Bob might be plenty, while two hours of Mary Poppins seems reasonable.

Zoë said, "Yeah, because Sponge Bob shows us his underwear and Mary Poppins doesn't."

The moral: if you haven't got a seven-year-old to watch movies with, borrow one.

Find Out What Your Life Means

"If your life doesn't demand a supernatural explanation, you haven't earned the right to be heard," Stephen Olford wrote.

When I came across this quote, it struck me as awfully true.

I've often asked myself, why in the heck should anybody care about my stories? And I've read lots of books, even some I've enjoyed, and asked myself at the end, "Why did I waste my time reading that? Did I learn anything from it? Did it change me in any way? Was it beautiful enough to lift my spirit? Did it move me to do something good?"

Our stories are commonly sparked by events we've witnessed or lived through or by people we've known or seen or heard of. The people or events often prompt our curiosity. We want to know more. So we write stories about them, and we bring other personal or vicarious experiences into the stories. And, if we've been honest, by the end we have become more enlightened.

When I was seventeen, my best friend Eric died in a car crash after making prophetic remarks about his death. Ever since, I've been writing about him in one disguise or another. Not about his actual life, but about what might have been, had he kept living. And in doing so, I've come slightly closer to satisfying my curiosity about some mysteries his real life posed.

During the early '70s, I was at a party in King's Beach on the shore of Lake Tahoe. On one side of the room was a group of folks smoking marijuana and guzzling beer. On the other side was a Bible study in progress.

In the middle of the room stood a girl who looked troubled. She kept glancing back and forth from one group to the other. After minutes of obvious dismay and confusion, she ran out of the house and straight down the road, and jumped into the cold lake, wearing jeans and a T-shirt. Being a snoop and a writer, I had followed her.

That event became the germ of a story, and she became the model for the main character of my novel *Midheaven*.

Midheaven also concerned some of the conflicts I had experienced while searching for my place in God's kingdom. Through telling the story, I came closer to fathoming the reasons why God allows the trials we encounter. And I hope some readers got the same benefit. If I didn't suspect there could be supernatural explanations for all I have lived through and seen, I might still write stories, but none of them would even begin to set anybody free. Me, least of all.

Give Thanks

In *The Brothers Karamazov*, brother Dmitri, while in jail awaiting prison, asks brother Alyosha: "If [brother] Ivan is right, if God doesn't exist, then who can we have to thank?"

I like to watch *Veggie Tales* with my little Zoë. My favorite episode is "Madame Blueberry," in which a young cucumber sings, "I give thanks for this day, for the sun in the sky, for my mom and my dad, for my piece of apple pie, for the love that we share, 'cause He listens to our prayers. That's why I give thanks every day." And here comes the best part: "Because a thankful heart is a happy heart."

I was driving north from San Diego to Manhattan Beach, near L.A., to teach at a writers' conference. On the way, I stopped to see my friend Alan Russell. He and I were supposed to have dinner that evening with Mike Connelly, a best-selling author friend of ours. Mike gets chauffeured around and sent on tours to Europe. But he's still a good guy.

I was going to miss the dinner because of this writing conference.

On the road to L.A., while sparring with a jillion motorists, I wrestled with disappointment that, instead of hanging out with Alan and Mike, I would be teaching so many classes I probably wouldn't find time to write. I had left home in the middle of a revision and had hoped to tackle it for a while every day, at least long enough to keep it active in my mind. But my mind was cluttered with such junk, I felt sour, worn out. Whatever the opposite of inspired is.

I put on an Andre Crouch CD. A song made me think about the cucumber's song. My thoughts turned to thankful ones, and before long, I was happily contemplating getting to this conference hotel. "Because a thankful heart is a happy heart."

Of course, being thankful, like all things spiritual, has to be done in love and humility, or else our crafty and self-favoring minds will warp it into something sinister.

In a Flannery O'Connor story, Ruby Turpin is in a doctor's waiting room looking around and thanking God she's not one of the coloreds or white trash, when an ugly girl calls her a warthog from hell. Which leads her, over some pages, to a vision of a procession into the sky, on the road to Heaven, and of herself at the tag end, far behind all the white trash and coloreds.

A kind of thanks I suspect God approves of isn't even so much a thank you for this or that at all, but more of a condition of heart.

The Brothers Karamazov's Father Zossima as a young man, after participating in a duel, has a revelation upon which the rest of his life will turn. To his companions: "'Gentlemen,' I cried suddenly, speaking straight from my heart, 'look around at the gifts of God, the clear sky, the pure air, the tender grass, the birds; nature is beautiful and sinless, and we, only we, are godless and foolish, and we don't understand that life is a paradise, for we have only to understand that and it will at once be fulfilled in all its beauty, and we shall embrace each other and weep.'"

Thanks, like most every good thing, requires us to love. And the more we learn to love, the more thankful we can be, and the happier.

From Saint Paul's letter to a congregation of Romans: "They were not thankful and they became vain in their imaginations and their foolish hearts were darkened."

Neither hearts nor minds can see in the dark.

Consider Yourself Responsible

I picked up a book, *What Nietzsche Really Said.* Overall, it's a valuable study, by some professors from Texas. But what follows, I balked at:

In defense of wicked acts either inspired by Nietzsche or justified by reference to him, the authors wrote, "Once again, we want to proclaim, rather indignantly, that an author is not responsible for vile misreadings of his works."

Okay, it would be silly to hold an author to blame for the extreme misreading of a theme or metaphor. But to give a writer absolute license to create without taking any responsibility is in a sense denying the power of language and image.

For example, the Beatle's *White Album* got some vile misreadings by Charles Manson. He perceived "Blackbird" as a call for him to spark a violent uprising by the black community, and at least one reason he engineered the Tate murders was so that white folks, blaming black folks, would take revenge, causing black folks to retaliate. That interpretation was truly nuts. But for him to accept the literal words of "Happiness is a Warm Gun" as a validation of his homicidal inclinations didn't require the slightest misreading of any kind.

If I ever bumped into those professors, I might

corner them and argue that while authors shouldn't plague themselves with guilt over potential misreadings, they most certainly should consider how their words might affect impressionable readers. And children aren't the only impressionable ones around.

Look Out

Jack Kerouac and plenty of his fellow writers of what got labeled the Beat Generation attempted to write directly from their unconscious minds, which may be a place where the Spirit (or spirits) resides. Like the Surrealists in France, the Beats often practiced free-writing, letting whatever wanted to come, come, refusing to let the conscious mind's editor block its way.

By this effort, the Beat writers not only helped define the 1950s but also played a lead role in instigating what we think of as the '60s. They initiated some primary themes of the hippie movement and launched in many hearts the quest for freedom from restraints which has since effected all manner of change. It certainly fueled the "sexual revolution" which has presented us with so many consequences, not the least the idolization of youth and vitality and disdain for the wisdom of age and experience.

When a spirit moves us, it's wise to recall the example of the Beats, or of Wagner or Nietzsche who've been accused of empowering Hitler. Those examples can remind us that art leads to consequences.

People in churches are often taught that the test of whether an inspiration comes from God is how well it lines up with Scripture. That's wise advice, but we authors will encounter inspirations to which that advice won't seem to apply.

Follow me through a weekend:

At the writer's conference in Manhattan Beach, at a Marriot, I taught the "Rogue Workshop," which starts at 9 p.m. and goes till the last student writer fades.

At one minute to 9, I left the Padre play-off game and went downstairs to teach. The workshop lasted a few hours. About 1 a.m. I flopped on my bed.

Now, I rarely go anywhere without a novel to read, because even if I have no other time, I read myself to sleep. But, I had forgotten to bring a novel. So I rifled through the drawers in the nightstands and found the Gideon. I turned to the end to see if it featured a concordance, since I wanted to look up the word "thanks," which had inspired me on the drive to this place, and see where all it's mentioned. But, no concordance. And since my search for a concordance took me to the end of the book and I was too weary to turn many pages and I hadn't the mind left over at this hour to tackle anything in Revelation, I flipped a few pages back to 1st John. And the last thing I read before I conked out was:

"Beloved, do not believe every spirit, but test the spirits, whether they are of God; because many false prophets have come into the world."

Spirits, I thought, and promised myself to jot a note about this in the morning, since the verse ought to give us confidence that we have the ability to discern between the angelic and the demonic, either of which may seek to inspire us.

About 7 a.m. I woke up and went out for coffee then returned to my room and sat in front of the television, which I almost never do. I looked for sports or news, to learn whether the Padres got bumped out of the playoffs last night. When I had left the game to teach the workshop, they were behind 5-0.

As I wielded the remote, and before I reached a sports or news channel, I landed on a sermon by Kenneth Copeland, who isn't my favorite kind of preacher. But no matter, he was preaching from 1st John, about the commandment Jesus gives us to love one another, and how our love proves our faith. 1st John again.

Organ music came on. I went looking for the Padre score. But I landed on another show that featured another preacher. A pretty blonde was questioning him. In response to one question, he assured her that God promises if we seek his will in humility and through prayer, he'll give us the right answers.

I didn't watch this guy for long because I found his toupee distracting. Besides, by now I was thinking I needed to write down this string of bits of advice I was tuning in to. I supposed I would conclude from them that if we ask in humility, with thanks and love, God will clue us which inspirations to use and which to ignore.

Then we needn't fear changing the world for the worse in our attempt to change it for the better. Because "There is no fear in love; but perfect love casts out fear." 1 John 4:18

five — Suggestions, Rants, Conclusions

Consider Olga

The vows of the Missionaries of Charity, Mother Teresa's order, are "poverty, chastity, obedience and wholehearted and free service to the poorest of the poor." The order also has lay members who take the same vow. In their case it means living modestly, reserving sex for marriage, following the guidance of a mentor, and serving the poor wherever and whenever feasible.

As artists, we'll be lots healthier if we think of ourselves as having taken a vow to cheerfully accept poverty if that's all the wealth we're given; to be chaste in our artistic vision (not be seduced by the commercial or trendy); and to be obedient in pursuing art, craft, and Spirit. If we live in such ways, our work will be of service.

My first class in graduate school at the University of Iowa was with John Irving. I remember an admonition he gave about money. He suggested that serious fiction writers should take an attitude like poets do, conceding that they're never going to make a living with their art and they need to support themselves some other way.

A couple years later, with *The World According to Garp*, Irving made a fortune. Which poses a problem for writers like me.

Sensible poets accept that writing poems alone won't support them, since hardly any poets make a living that way. But more than a few fiction writers make heaps of money, so even the sensible among us may hope to cash in.

Alan Russell and I were on a radio show with Tess Gerritsen, who turned from medicine to writing thrillers. Offstage, Alan asked Tess if she ever regretted giving up doctoring. She said, "Well, you can make more money writing."

I choked on my gum.

For a couple years I wrote a weekly column for the *San Diego Reader*. The nominal topic was people and their cars. Here's one:

Even Texan George Bush talked about conservation and cutting our reliance on oil. So I'm convinced it's time we ask ourselves if living more like Olga Savitsky wouldn't be preferable to the way we're living.

Olga's a minimalist. Though plenty educated (holding a Master of City Planning degree) and able to follow a more lucrative career, she chooses to work only a few short days a week cleaning houses. She shares an apartment and pays less than $400 for rent and utilities, in a pleasant neighborhood near a commercial district. On most of her errands, she can walk. When she needs to drive, she uses her 1994 Toyota Tercel.

She tells me, "It's not like a sacrifice. I just don't need much. A person with a family needs more than I do. Usually what somebody needs depends upon their function. A corporate CEO, maybe he's got to throw parties and he needs a bigger house. But I don't throw parties, so what good is a big house to me? The only reason I'd want one is because the media tells me I ought to have one. We see all this stuff and the desire to have some gets aroused and commercials come on and convince us we need it all, and so on, until we're beyond debt and into distress."

Olga wears jeans and T-shirts. "That's all I own. They're comfortable, they last. I just bought two new pairs of jeans for $16 each, and they'll last two years. To me, the key to living well is living in a way that gives an opportunity for appreciating nature and friends and taking time for prayer and writing and helping people. And unless you inherit a pile of money, the way to live like that is to not want a lot of stuff. Most stuff is just clutter. But our culture feeds the desire to own or consume until what we think we need makes us greedy.

"The Bible says that we should work so we'll have something to share with people in need. I can work for a few days a week cleaning houses and by not letting myself want a bunch of stuff, I can have money to give away. So I'm careful about what I buy, and I pick the things I do buy for durability and longevity. I need a car, so I buy a Toyota. If I needed a car that would break down, I could buy a Jaguar.

"And it isn't only the desire for stuff that devours our time. It's also that we try to buy security. People think they need to not only have lots of stuff, but to save or invest or buy some insurance so they'll be sure they'll always have lots of stuff. We need a bit more faith. I mean, I don't have AAA or any kind of roadside service insurance because every time a car of mine has broken down, it's been a block or so from my mechanic's house. Except one time.

"The one time my car broke down in an inconvenient place, a guy stopped to help me, and he happened to be the handsomest man I ever saw. Maybe he was an angel. I don't know. But it sure was fun breaking down."

Remember Olga

Søren Kierkegaard contended that belief based on evidence isn't faith at all, because faith is from a source other than our reasoning minds. Belief based on experience is reason. And what God wants us to have is faith.

In college, I changed my major from Philosophy to English because I found encountering new ideas more exciting than debating them. So I'll take Kierkegaard's words to heart because they feel true, and I'll apply the idea of faith independent of experience to writing.

Olga, while battling cancer, one Sunday in church explained that faith is something we all have, but it often applies only to certain parts of our lives. We may have faith about our finances, that what we need will always arrive. We may have faith in our friends or family, that they'll stick by us, no matter what.

Olga contended that we should recognize the faith we have, notice how it may run counter to the weight of our experience and observations, and consider the benefits of peace and security it gives us. God, she argued, wants us to extend that faith into other areas and to trust that he can and will heal us, even though evidence might run counter to such faith.

From which I'll reason that God wants us writers to

extend our faith into our vocations and trust that we have the necessary gifts and are on our way to becoming masterful writers no matter if every publisher on earth has insulted and rejected us, or though everyone in our critique group has said or implied we're hopeless.

Such faith can be dangerous. If it seems to fail, say we pray for Olga and she doesn't get healed, we may begin to doubt God or our own judgment. At these times it helps to return to Kierkegaard and remember that belief based on evidence isn't faith at all, that faith comes from elsewhere, perhaps from the Spirit.

Even when it seems to fail, faith has enriched our experience. And writing, like faith, should be judged by the value of the process, not only by the results. So if we've worked on a novel for ten years, if the process has enriched us, who are we to gripe when no publisher wants it?

Faithful work is always going to enrich us, since exercising faith, even in one area such as writing, builds a stronger faith we can apply to other areas, such as public speaking. Or parenting, or healing. Because faith isn't a mental quirk. Like Saint Paul tells us, it's a substance.

Lower Your Standards

After reading the title above, you might say, "Huh? Didn't this crazy fellow advise us to become perfect and to do our best?"

Okay, but consistency's the mark of a stagnant mind. Besides, Solomon claimed there's a time for every purpose.

Students ask me how to overcome writer's block. I tell them writer's block doesn't exist. In fact, if anybody in my proximity mentions writer's block, I jump in and tell them it doesn't exist.

Anybody who has learned to read and make letters can at any time sit down and write. What paralyzes some of us is the inability to decide what to write about, or to think of words that express our thoughts precisely.

The obvious solution is: Write what comes to mind, and if it doesn't delight you with its wit, passion, profundity or relevance to the project you want it to work in, take comfort in the fact that most of what any of us write is lousy, or at least flawed. Which is why we learn to revise. After time enough passes so that we can read our words with a fresh eye, and after we cut, fill in, allow for new inspiration, what started as blah blah blah may transform into something that weaves a spell.

And once we grow confident that with patience we

can take a mediocre page and make it a good one, we'll never have to pester anybody with questions about how to overcome writer's block.

Pam, Zoë's mom, between kindergarten and college, never received a grade below an "A". She missed only one day of school, and that was because she decided to avoid the second half of a film about the End Times, which the entire school was obliged to watch (Tim LaHaye, of *Left Behind* fame, was a founder of the school), because the first half had terrified her.

Pam is a perfectionist, but she's trying to change, because she has learned that driving herself so hard tends to burns her out and causes trauma that makes her a less effective and less happy person. Better to live and work at a steady pace, even if it has required giving up her dream of becoming the youngest full professor ever or her ambition of throwing Zoë a world class birthday party on a budget.

But suppose the master painter I quoted some pages back is correct, and to write the perfect story (or scene, or image) we need to become perfect.

Well, we'll never get perfect by driving ourselves. Our only chance of becoming perfect lies in the effort to shed everything that will keep us from letting the Spirit fill our hearts with joy, peace, patience, self-control, kindness, goodness, faithfulness, gentleness, and love.

Simplify

At every college in which I've taught creative writing, I've found the Journalism majors are usually the best fiction writers, and often the best poets.

One reason is, Journalism majors are taught to write for people who may not be as literate as they are. They're taught to make their points and paint their pictures clearly.

Meanwhile, Literature and Creative Writing majors strive to be profound, often before they've become good, or even sensible, let alone wise.

When Dana passed along Michael Seidman's advice that for commercial books, a sentence should be between eight and twelve words long, a paragraph no more than nine lines, I thought about those Journalism majors.

It happened that my current bedtime reading was Michael Connelly's novel *The Closers*. I knew Mike had been a Journalism major and a reporter even though he realized early on that his goal was to write fiction.

Mike and I have a history together. We entered the mystery community about the same time and did our share of signings together. Mike has gotten ever more rich and famous. I haven't.

Hmmm, I thought, after I read Seidman's dictum. I

wonder if part of the reason Connelly's on the best-seller list and I'm not is that he majored in Journalism and I majored in Literature.

So I read *The Closers* with an eye to sentence lengths. Though I found lots of sentences that exceeded Seidman's standards, I also realized that every one of them was clear. Never did I have to reread a sentence.

Contemplating Seidman's rule led me to the truth that any kind of commercial fiction needs to read so clearly that words, or grammar, or sentence structure won't interrupt or break the fictional dream but will allow the reader to press on without going back to reread.

The best writers clarify the obscure and simplify the complex.

So I'll suggest that writers who came from literature backgrounds consider posting this reminder in giant letters near their writing station: MAKE IT SIMPLE AND CLEAR.

Ask For It

I had been on a book signing tour in the northwest. My son Cody flew to meet me in Sacramento for a few days of camping.

Even as an adult, Cody's not an avid talker, and at fourteen, he could've passed for a mute. Yet before we drove many miles from the airport, he told me he'd been reading the Bible and that a couple proverbs convinced him fools shun guidance and correction but wise people go out looking for advice.

That comment blessed me with the joy that arose from my realizing my son was on his way to a bountiful life.

As writers, beyond learning how to live with rejection and criticism, we need to seek out criticism, even though it may feel like rejection. Because we're trying to communicate, we must ask people how well we've communicated our ideas, our passions and emotions, our world-view.

But read on.

Trust Nobody

Everybody who reads your work is liable to respond differently. Even in a group of smart, knowledgeable writers or editors, you might get responses ranging from abject boredom to wild acclaim.

The graduate school I attended is famous, so good writers apply. I went there expecting that most every participant in the workshops would give me wise insights. Most of them didn't.

But I didn't need the comments of fifteen people. From the critiques of two or three with whom I felt some accord, I learned plenty.

Everybody brings his background to his reading. When a reader appreciates my work, I know it could mean he relates for his own reasons. Say we both were raised by our grandmothers. Or she may dismiss my story in reaction to something personal, such as a hurt she suffered or a bias with which she has armed herself. A person who grew up with alcoholic parents may bond with a story about a boozer or recoil from it.

The odds of an agent or editor accepting a book she reads over coffee in the morning may be higher than the odds of her buying one she reads in moments snatched between phone calls.

Suppose several readers point to the same problem.

Odds are good your story has failed to communicate the way you'd like it to. But that doesn't mean the readers' suggestions for fixing the problem are correct. They're worth considering, but not necessarily the best way to solve the problem.

When critiquing an early draft of a novel by Kevin McIlvoy, I noted that a certain section dragged along, earning more yawns than the rest of the story. I suggested cutting some details to speed it up. Kevin later told me he'd solved the problem by adding to the section, using more details that made it more gripping.

Your task is to listen to critiques with your mind open, then ponder each comment as much as it deserves, all before you decide whether to revise. And if you decide to revise, consider suggestions, but also look for alternative ways. Suggestions can come from other people, but revisions have to come from you.

Get to the Bottom of It

Rules don't matter. What does matter is the reason for the rule.

If you ever teach a freshman composition class and assign a formal essay, you'll find that about half the students believe they can't use the word "I."

It's a fact that in student essays, the "I" can intrude, but that's not because it's a bad word. It's because the usage will be something like "I think" or "I believe," which adds nothing since we can presume that a writer making a statement means she thinks or believes it. But apparently many teachers don't bother with reasons, only with rules.

Adverbs are currently out of fashion. Because of this, some editors and writing teachers have made "no adverbs" a rule. But in doing so, they're snatching away a useful tool. Better to advocate restraint and explain that adverbs fell out of fashion because too many sloppy writers substituted a weak verb and an adverb for a strong verb, which is most always sharper, more vivid.

Every time we encounter a rule, let's contemplate until we discover the reason for the rule.

If we know a rule and apply it without under-standing, we have discarded a tool from our magic kit. If we know the reason for it, we have discarded nothing.

Rather, we have found and now possess another tool.

Listen

Saint Paul wrote to a group of Galatians, "You, my brothers, were called to be free. But do not use your freedom to indulge the sinful nature; rather, serve one another in love."

Charlie Gregg wrote, "Love is listening. To practice listening is to practice serving. To practice serving is to practice loving. Listening carries faith and hope. If I am listening fully to another person, it presupposes that they may have something from which I can benefit. This is the opposite of disdain. When I neglect to listen, to be fully present, I am non-verbally communicating the message that the person speaking has nothing of value for me at this particular time. Listening is Honor. One writer called it the queen of all compliments."

He closes with a quote from Sue Patton. "Deep listening is miraculous for both listener and speaker. When someone receives us with open-hearted, non-judging, intensely interested listening, our spirits expand."

Listening to people gives us the obvious benefits of the opportunity to build our dialogue-writing skills, and allows us to study how other people think. Listening to our characters, both heroes and villains, helps bring them to life.

Listening also gives us a chance to practice love.

Olga knew the Bible. She had read and studied Scripture or commentaries most every day for thirty-some years, and she was a bright and conscientious student, the valedictorian of her high school graduating class, and her memory was remarkable. Yet every time we talked about Biblical stuff, though she knew the Bible lots better than I do, she would listen and gently agree or disagree, or else decline to give an opinion. Because she knew that truth is illusive; that we can learn from the wise, the foolish and the in-between; and that our calling isn't so much to convince or educate people as to love them.

And the more we practice love and learn to love better, the more effectively we can apply love to our work.

Besides, the better we listen, the more we can understand the human heart, which is, after all, the essential subject of most every remarkable story.

Pay Attention

A master violinist spent time in a subway station playing an intricate piece on a violin worth millions. But few people paid him or his music any attention.

We artists need to pay attention.

But many of our heads are spinning too fast to allow us to stop and look. No doubt we could benefit from practicing some of the attentiveness meditation that's popular these days, unless the idea of practicing anything else than what we're already doing sends us into quakes of horror.

Lately, I've been writing, running Perelandra College where I also teach, and raising my amazing Zoë largely on my own. I'm determined she'll stay happy and as innocent as one can be in a perilous world, and that she'll grow up emotionally, mentally, spiritually, and financially able to pursue whatever she's called to.

All these tasks are privileges for which I'm grateful and which give me joy, but they don't leave much time to pay attention to the sunsets or old shoes Raymond Carver would have us view with amazement.

I could quit running the college, or teaching, and when the time's right, I will. Meanwhile I often remind myself of the way my friend Bob cooks and washes dishes, at a leisurely clip, as though he'd as just as soon be doing those chores as anything else. The only way we busy folks can wash dishes without rushing is to convince ourselves that the other chores on our agenda aren't as urgent as we've considered them.

Us Christians are advised that the only crucial chore is communing with God. Besides, in all but rare cases, the key to succeeding with our goals, whether they be clean kitchens or novels, isn't urgency but persistence.

Linger on That Thought

I like to go to church Friday evenings, in part to recover from the week, and because our church is less crowded, calmer than on Sundays. But since my son Cody attends on Sundays, I've been returning to hang out with him.

Occasionally, the pastor tosses in something new on Sunday, but most of the message is the same as Friday's. Which has led to a solution of a problem of mine. The problem is, when I listen to a sermon or a lecture or a poem or song or whatever, a line or idea grabs me and I follow it, and often get lost and miss the next part of whatever.

What I've discovered is, knowing I'll be listening twice allows my mind to work in two different ways. On Fridays, I'm like a dutiful student, filling in the blanks on the outline, doing my best to take in the message for what it is, not what my wandering mind will make of it. On Sundays, I let lines or ideas in the message take me wherever, which usually leads to my scribbling notes about stories or other projects of mine.

These days, with downloads of sermons and lectures readily available, lingering on those with substance, listening two or three times from different approaches, might convince the Spirit that we are paying attention and deserving of a gift.

Pray

One of the stories in *Kesey's Garage Sale*, a collection of this and that by novelist Ken Kesey, is an autobiographical piece about the author's son getting mangled in an auto wreck. Kesey goes to the hospital and, after being told the kid is dead, prays for him to revive. The kid revives, and Kesey closes the story with a suggestion that some night when we're in our cabin and have settled down before a fire to smoke a joint, we might want to try reading the Bible.

Prayer is a mysterious business. People often warn, "Be careful what you pray for." But that advice may only apply if you're trying to avoid trials and tribulation.

A visiting speaker at our church told a harrowing story. As a young man, he lived in a Christian commune and worked as a handyman. He was on a roof, taking down an antenna, when the antenna hit a high voltage wire and killed him. Then God brought him back to life.

That very morning, he had prayed for God to use him. And ever since the accident (or whatever it was), the story and the physical scars--still apparent years after the weeks he spent receiving skin grafts--have been his calling card and the heart of the message he uses to evangelize.

In my early twenties, I took a job teaching at a small

school in a camp for boys on probation. Most of them belonged to L.A. and Compton gangs. The school was an hour's drive from my home, and the job required special training in teaching literacy, as many of the boys could hardly read.

Months of five school days each week, and Saturdays at the camp doing reports and such, along with the drive and two evenings each week of college classes in Developmental Reading, left me emotionally wrung out, devoid of joy, love, or even hope.

My friend Laurent came to visit on his way to cross the country to propose to a girl and start medical school. He was so elated, so intense in pursuit of his goals, seeing him like that drove me to lock myself in my room and pray. I asked God to give me emotional intensity.

The next day, boys at the camp revolted. They harvested morning glory seeds and Jimson weed and used them, as well as gasoline and paint thinner fumes, to get loaded. They beat the camp's pet pig to death with sticks, stole guns from a neighboring house, and set fire to one of the camp's cabins.

A few days after the revolt, I got stricken by what doctors refer to as panic disorder. Never again, God assured me, would my emotional life be less than intense.

Before long, I knew plenty more about the terrors people in crisis may suffer.

Writers need such knowledge. Dostoyevski might never have written his masterpieces if he hadn't gotten imprisoned in Siberia. I wonder if he landed there as the result of prayer.

I mean these anecdotes neither as advice nor warnings, only to suggest that we shouldn't underestimate the power of fervent prayer.

Don't Wait for the Spirit to Move You

One of the benefits of prayer is that it can either quiet our minds or open them and allow the Spirit a time to speak to us. Writing can do the same. Whether we're tickling the keyboard or taking a meditative walk or staring into space with a story drifting in and out of our minds, the process can open a door for the Spirit to enter.

People have told me they would love to try writing but they have nothing important or unique to say. Other people believe they have plenty to say but question their ability to write.

All those people are misguided. What they need to do, if they want to write, is begin. Because the elements of a story, poem, essay or song often appear, all at once or little by little, while we are working. When a simple idea for a character, a setting, or a conflict meets the mental and emotional processes we employ as we write.

Most story writers feel that the stories themselves teach them what they want to say. And the skill to express what you mean comes with experience. Which every minute spent writing adds to.

I mean, no matter what you hope to create, waiting is usually procrastination, and a waste of precious time.

When in Danger, Write

If I didn't have any other reasons to write novels, this one would be plenty: For the past few months, life has been treacherous. When I'm doing chores, driving, trying to sleep, cooking or picking up after Zoë (I know she ought to pick up after herself), pursuing any task but writing, my mind whirls, besieged by questions and concerns.

A while back, my friend Mark told me he planned to start writing again once he'd worked out some family and financial issues. He said he couldn't write with all that on his mind. I replied that most writers, if they waited for respites from such issues, would never finish a book.

One solid piece of wisdom I've picked up: as long as we're thinking about our selves and our concerns, we're in grave danger of becoming distressed and miserable. When we turn to thinking about other people, we rise above that distress and at least have a chance to feel the emergence of joy.

Similarly, writing takes us out of ourselves. When I travel from the present to live in 1935, or whenever my current story is set, and to become someone else or my own alter-ego and contend with a gang of fascinating characters, the present, with all its fears, worries and dilemmas, can't reach me.

In that world of imagination, I am free.

Get Help

1.

During a time when my writing career felt futile, a friend sent me to a place called the Healing Room.

A young man and an older woman asked what I needed. I told them I was a discouraged writer.

They felt inspired to read scriptures to me.

One from Genesis: "In the course of time Cain brought to the Lord an offering of the fruit of the ground, and Abel for his part brought the firstlings of his flock, their fat portions. And the Lord had regard for Abel and his offering, but for Cain and his offering he had no regard."

One from Luke: "He said to them, 'The harvest is plentiful but the laborers are few; therefore ask the Lord of the harvest to send out laborers into his harvest. Go on your way. See, I am sending you out like lambs into the midst of wolves."

One from Jeremiah: "Call me and I will answer you, and will tell you great and hidden things that you have not known."

And one from Isaiah: "The spirit of the Lord is upon me, because the Lord has anointed me, to provide for those who mourn in Zion, to give them a garland instead of ashes, the oil of gladness instead of mourning, the mantle of praise instead of a faint spirit."

2.

That afternoon I drove over the mountains and across the desert to visit my Darcy, her husband Darren, and my grandson Nick in Tucson.

I put in a CD by Barry McGuire and Terry Talbot. As I listened to a cover of the Beatles' "Help," I recalled the passage from Genesis and realized something I hadn't thoroughly grasped before about Cain. I saw that God didn't accept Cain's sacrifice because it was what Cain wanted to give, not what God wanted from him. Maybe, I thought, Cain didn't know what God wanted him to give. And maybe he didn't know because he didn't ask and wait for the answer.

Perhaps I was writing what I wanted to write and not what God wanted me to. Or even, perhaps God wanted me to give up writing in favor of something else. That last thought horrified me.

A couple songs later came one that starts with the lyric, "I can't call you Lord and then not obey you," and goes on to petition God, "Speak to me, I will obey." Which reinforced the Cain lesson and added a footnote that led to Jeremiah's prophesy, "Call me and I will answer you, and will tell you great and hidden things that you have not known." Maybe, should I more frequently call on him, God would give my stories more wisdom.

The man in the Healing Rooms had told me he felt a pervasive heaviness, as if I were laboring under a great burden. He asked what gave me joy, and I realized I hadn't been feeling a lot of joy.

A song called "A'Soulin'" is about roving moochers around Christmas time. Toward the end, in the Talbot-McGuire version, a child's voice comes in singing "God Rest Ye Merry Gentlemen." The last line is "tidings of comfort and joy." When I heard the word joy, I realized that the source of the deepest comfort and joy I have ever known is when I feel as if I am living and working in God's will.

Some years ago, I wrote a magazine story about priests and seminarians in Tijuana with the Missionaries of Charity, Mother Teresa's order. Dean McFalls, a seminarian, showed me around. In the chapel, over the altar, a larger than life Christ hung from his cross. At his feet stood a small woman dressed in Missionaries of Charity garb. According to the caption, Christ was saying "*Tengo sed.*" In English that's "I thirst." The woman was handing Jesus a cup of water.

Dean said, "That's how we define what we're doing. Mother doesn't think of us as ministering to people but as ministering to Christ in his distressing disguise."

Later, I was helping the brothers pass out food to some poor folks, and marveling at how happy I felt. Afterward, I told Dean that even though I hadn't come to help anybody and was only pursuing a story and making money, I felt blessed.

Dean said, "When you minister to Christ in his distressing disguise, he blesses you back many times over."

The six-hour drive across the desert following my trip to the Healing Room felt like the trip of a lifetime, like a cruise to a land where I was greeted with "a garland instead of ashes, the oil of gladness instead of mourning, the mantle of praise instead of a faint spirit."

Which may only prove I'm at least slightly deranged and have more imagination than sense. Or it may be evidence of grace.

Be Quiet

Author Anne LeClair chose to be silent for twenty-four hours at least twice a month. She says it helps her hear herself and her characters. Her reflections on the experience can be found in her book, *Listening Below the Noise: A Meditation on the Practice of Silence.*

In an interview she talks about a walk on the beach during a day when her best friend's mother was dying and she was in a tender place. "When we're tenderhearted," she said, "we open to the universe [God, in my vocabulary], which is one of the roles grief plays in our life, and I thought about the many things I was grateful for. I thought, I love my husband, friends, and I have enormous privilege of doing what I do for a living. It's not as if I haven't known loss and grief but even that I'm grateful for because of what it's taught me. As I was thinking about this I teared up. I didn't know what do. A man behind me on the beach said, 'Sit in silence.' I turned around and there was no one there. Nothing like that has ever happened before or since. It was so profound and real it called me to attention. What could that mean? And I thought maybe it just means: Be quiet."

She decided to spend the next day in silence, and discovered that her writing that day was smooth and focused. "I heard things in myself that normally there's too much chatter to hear." The day slowed down in a way she describes as delicious. At day's end, she felt restored and rested.

But the next time she devoted a day to silence, old sorrows appeared and she came to realize that when the noise stops, whatever we have been running from will catch up. Silence doesn't always bring peace, but it rarely fails to give us something of value. "Silence taught me to listen to myself and to the people around me and to my characters."

Get Lost

Fabre d'Olivet, in a strange and fascinating old book called *The Hermeneutic Interpretation of the Origin of the Social State of Man*, contended that: "Only in the heat of battle did the ancient Celts, besieged on all sides by demons, find a sort of repose."

I must have met a lot of the ancient Celts' descendants. Either I attract them, or they attract me, or they're everywhere.

Ever since I felt called to write, I've dreamed of a retreat, a trailer in the desert, a mountain cabin.

When I'm at home, no sooner have I landed in the zone, than a friend calls to report on some tragedy, or Zoë comes wanting to bake and we have run out of butter. I spend a few minutes with my friend then run to the market and afterward attempt to pick up where I left off. Sometimes I am able.

But too many interruptions can sour my spirit, dim my hope, and lure demons out of the labyrinth. Then, every phrase I put together might strike me as verbal slop, and every thought can feel like trivia.

The pastor at our church recommends that our process of growing closer to God can benefit from times of solitude, and he tells about a hideaway in the desert, which some nice parishioners lend him.

Okay. I'm pleased he's gets to do that.

But imagine a single mom or dad with no friends who own and offer a desert retreat. What's this person to do if his or her mind or emotions or art could use a healthy jolt of solitude? How should we answer this person's rant, "Yeah, well just how and where am I supposed to get quiet when the house is a mess and the bills need paying, and the car's broken, and the kids are bugging me to coach the soccer team, and so on?"

Go to the desert, I suggest.

I mean, a couple days, a few hours, or even some minutes may be all you need. Camp out. Stay at the Motel 6, wherever you don't know anybody.

Or an hour a week in the park might be enough, or a monthly walk in the woods or along some lakeshore. Or, if you can send the family to your in-laws for a few days, unplug the phone and invite the spirit to come visit your home.

Every school day morning I walk Zoë down the hill. Yesterday I extended the walk to take me to a business meeting at a coffee house. Half way there, a momentous inspiration came, a clear vision of the hearts and minds of the five crucial characters in a novel with which I have been wrestling since way back when my hair was full, dark, and long.

I vowed to extend my morning walk at least once a week.

If I run out of ideas that excite me and a walk or a

drive across the desert doesn't leave me inspired, I'll make a trip to Lake Tahoe, where the peace and heavenly air might enable the Spirit to reach me with enough material to last several years.

But suppose the Spirit stands me up. Even so, I get a glorious trip out of the deal.

Be Ridiculous

1.

Since my years in graduate school, writing programs have proliferated and produced thousands of technically excellent writers. But these programs, being mostly workshops, too often promote such attention to detail it eviscerates stories. Writers may learn to so fear being labeled melodramatic, flowery or sentimental they avoid topics that are dearest to them.

A few years ago, I served as a judge for an Arizona Commission on the Arts Literary Fellowship competition. I read about a hundred stories and was both impressed and appalled. Because about ninety of the submissions were masterfully written, in terms of language and style. But only three even began to move me. And I'm a pushover for stories.

Once, in a review for *Literary Magazine Review,* I wrote that the reason I admired *Puerto del Sol* was that the editors appeared to choose stories for what was good in them rather than for their consistent competence, and for the effect of the story rather than the refinement.

2.

I've thought of myself as a Christian since I got

called to the altar at a Billy Graham crusade when I was nineteen. But I didn't approve of churches until twenty some years later when I felt God telling me to attend one. Then I learned to love the church I chose for many reasons. The pastor's wise and honest messages. The people who let their hearts get exposed. But the most glorious reason was that through grace aided by words, music, and human kindness, the assurance of God's love lifted the burden of my past, snatching away the guilt for my mistakes and selfish actions.

Christ set us free from the law that condemns, right? Which means we should live free from guilt.

I have a number of friends, some of them writers, who suffer from depression that appears to have risen straight from the guilt imposed upon them as children in Christian families.

Regarding our lives on this side of the grave, what's the point of believing if we're going to live in the guilt Christ sacrificed to free us from? I suppose some would argue that it makes us act in less harmful ways, but I don't see a lot of evidence for any such conclusion.

Here's an attitude that helps me keep largely free from guilt. I am a person. People are selfish. Therefore I am selfish. But I can, with the help of the Spirit, rise above my selfishness, and learn to love better. And I can forgive myself as God would have me forgive others.

3.

In his essay "Meditation and Poetry." Alan Ginsberg advises writers not to conform to their idea of what is expected but to conform to their present, spontaneous minds, to their raw awareness. He suggests that those who follow his advice will find they require de-conditioning of rigidity before they can arrive at their own thought. The de-conditioning can be aided by the meditative process of letting go of thoughts, only watching them arise and pass rather than engaging with them. Ginsberg urges writers to allow their minds to accept contradictions, paradoxes and mysteries, rather than to aggressively grasp for answers.

He quotes U.S. President John Adams: "The mind must be loose." He encourages artists to have the confidence to let loose of their minds and observe their perceptions and their discontinuities, and he contends that the life of meditation and the life of art are both based on allowing or achieving a spontaneous mind, as a way to follow Ezra Pound's dictum: "Make it new."

He urges writers to trust in "the magic of chance" which I might call the generosity of the spirit that moves us.

4.

Not long ago, in a single week I encountered several discussions of introverts and extroverts. I even took a survey and found myself high on the introvert side of the scale. But I'm not sure if introversion is my nature or if I simply choose the introvert's way of living because it often protects me from feeling ridiculous. If I go to a party or other gathering and fail to maintain my defenses, I'm in danger of lying in bed that night counting the instances when I have said things that might prompt somebody to consider me ridiculous.

Since I'm a fanatic about *The Brothers Karamazov*, I'll offer here advice brother Alyosha gives when a friend asks, "'Karamazov, tell me, am I very ridiculous now?'

"'Don't think about that, don't think of it at all!' cried Alyosha. 'And what does ridiculous mean? Isn't everyone constantly being or seeming ridiculous? Besides, nearly all clever people now are fearfully afraid of being ridiculous, and that makes them unhappy. Nowadays, the very children have begun to suffer from it. It's almost a sort of insanity. The devil has taken the form of that vanity and entered a whole generation; it's simply the devil.'"

Count it All Progress

One of my bad habits is assessing the value of each day as it passes by what tasks I've accomplished. Someday I may kick the habit entirely. For now, though, I'm going to alter it, on account of a realization.

I realized that the tasks don't matter so much as the good ideas that come.

When we analyze stories, we're wise to consider the climax as the turning point, and not as an action but as the thought or decision that propels the character toward the actions that determine her fate.

Likewise, a valuable accomplishment won't happen unless a good idea sets it into motion.

Now, a good idea isn't worth much unless it's somehow acted upon. Lots of folks are flooded with good ideas and intentions to bring the ideas to life but never find the motivation to proceed.

But for those of us obsessed with carrying out what good ideas we're given, if we don't accomplish a single task during a given day, so what? The tasks will get done by and by.

Besides, this outlook makes me feel lighter.

Know Your Reader

I'm a fan of Kinky Friedman's songs. He writes and performs such country classics as "They Ain't Makin' Jews Like Jesus Anymore." My favorite of his songs is "The People Who Read *People* Magazine."

One verse goes: "If you're too New York for Texas, too Texas for L.A./ You've been chasing trends like rainbow ends and you're always just a song away/ If the White House wouldn't have you, play at every little honkytonk and bar/ The good Lord made the heavens, but he never made a star/ It's the people who read *People* Magazine/ it's the soap opry lovers, it's the home town bowling team/ it's everybody everywhere who's ever lost a dream ..." And in another verse, he sings, "... if anyone should ask you, here's who I'm singing for/ It's the people who read People Magazine ..."

Get it? It's the people who read *People* that make entertainers into stars. Kinky knows his audience.

We all should be so conscious.

Prepare for the Exam

During the final months of her masterpiece of a life, Olga competed with her long-time best friend Warren Larkin in what they called an *agapeo* contest. *Agapeo* means selfless love of the kind God has for us.

To love, we need to give of ourselves. To give of ourselves, we need to be who we honestly are. We need to get real.

To get real takes plenty of courage. And courage, according to Nietzsche and me, is the will to overcome fear.

My teenage years were blighted by death. My dad, my best friend Eric Curtis, two other friends and a girl I dated, four uncles, an aunt, two grandparents.

When Eric died, I was seventeen and I vowed to hold myself distant enough from people so their death or desertion wouldn't hurt deeply.

For about a dozen years, I lived like that. Then my first little girl was born and the frozen sea inside me broke (thanks to Franz Kafka for that metaphor). Every day since, I've spent at least some time worrying about my kids, being afraid that perhaps, as Madame Clavel (the nun in the kids' books about Madeline) would say, "Something is not right." But as they are my greatest joy, and they've taught me how to love far better than I could have without them, I'm willing to accept the fear.

Besides, as Saint John proclaimed, "Perfect love casts out fear." So, rather than trying to dispel my fear, I'll keep trying to love better.

"The Good Samaritan" teaches us to love through action.

A couple years ago, Pam left Zoë and me. I won't presume to challenge or pretend to fully understand her reasons. But I will note that it's no cinch trying to do justice to raising a wonderful daughter as a single dad with only a modest income and with two demanding jobs. Sometimes, I was inclined toward resentment.

Each time Pam showed up, I would remind myself that, as Kierkegaard makes clear in *Works of Love*, I am called to love without distinction. Regardless of my feelings, I am obliged to act toward her in a loving way. To treat her with kindness, generosity, and concern.

Hold on, I thought, she did me ... *Whoa*, says the cartoon angel on my shoulder, *you're looking for a loophole*. Yeah, but if I treat her well, aren't I condoning ... *Whoa, loophole.*

A most unexpected and peculiar revelation came out of this practice. I began to see that resentment fades in light of a call to action. I experienced a strange release from resentment, a sense of freedom that felt like a gift or blessing. And freedom is a point of entry for the Spirit.

Lighten Up

"To allow oneself to be carried away by a
multitude of conflicting concerns,
to surrender oneself to too many demands,
to commit oneself to too many projects,
to want to help everyone in everything
is to succumb to violence.
More than that, it is cooperation in violence.
It destroys your own inner capacity for peace.
It destroys the fruitfulness of your own work,
because it kills the root of inner wisdom which
makes the work fruitful." Thomas Merton

When I read this on the wall of a doctor's office, it not only offered a key to inspiration but also gave a prerequisite.

Of all the attitudes, habits and challenges I prescribe, none can lead us any closer to the Spirit unless we find and take the time to write in peace.

Some of us can find peace even in the midst of turmoil.

Others of us need to structure our lives in ways that allow external peace to prevail, or to find us when we choose to create.

Thomas Merton found his peace in a monastery.

Every day, let's ask how or where can we find more peace.

Get to Work

Pastor Bart Hughes preached a sermon in which he contended that taking in from God but not giving out makes us like stagnant pools, when we could be fragrant streams. Because God means for us to take in and give out.

After all, "We are God's art, created in Christ Jesus *to do works of beauty*, which God has prepared in advance for us to do."

In his journals, Kierkegaard warns, "It is very dangerous to go into eternity with possibilities which one has oneself prevented from becoming realities. A possibility is a hint from God. One must follow it. In every one there is latent the highest possibility, and one must follow it. If God does not wish it then let God prevent it, but one must not hinder oneself. Trusting to God I have dared, but I was not successful; in that is to be found peace, calm, and confidence in God. I have not dared: that is a woeful thought, a torment in eternity."

six — I pretend to be omniscient

Dostoyevski?

In hopes of enlightening myself and some readers, I'm going to pretend to know everything that went into the creation of Feodor Dostoyevski's *The Brothers Karamazov*.

After all the times I've mentioned Dostoyevski, and since *The Brothers Karamazov* is the literary masterpiece I most admire, I feel obliged to probe more deeply into that book and its author.

When I taught at California State University, Chico, a bright student sent me to *The Hermeneutic Interpretation of the Origin of the Social States of Man*.

Hundreds of years ago, Fabre d'Olivet wrote the entire history of civilization by using inspiration or imagination to fill in the blanks in the record of history he learned from other sources.

I'm going to work like that, imagining (or using inspiration, should the Spirit appear), the preconditions of heart, mind, circumstance and attitude under which I might, had I the skill, wisdom and courage, write a book as powerful and blessed with inspiration as *The Brothers Karamazov*.

Before we attempt anything a tenth as ambitious as *The Brothers Karamazov*, we need to recall that Dostoyevski had already mastered the art of dramatic writing. His every scene features a character seeking to achieve a goal. By the end of each scene, the character has suffered what writers call a setback, a reversal or a disaster.

A dozen years ago, Gene Riehl retired from the FBI in order to write novels. He found a writers' group, read dozens of books on structure and other elements of fiction, mystery and suspense. After ten years of hard work, his first novel came out. His second book followed it. But then, for a year, he didn't write anything, and he saw no point in writing what he called "just another story."

One evening, I mentioned to Gene my admiration at how well Dostoyevski set up dramatic situations in which he could have his characters debate the issues he found most important. Gene sat up taller. "Do you think I could get away with doing that?"

"Try it," I said, only hoping his mastery of dramatic writing was sufficient.

My point is, unless you're a master dramatist, don't venture far from the spine of your story.

*

From the beginning, in his choice of a narrator, Dostoyevski assumes an attitude meant to summon the spirit that moves us.

He poses as an unpretentious, anonymous townsperson, who ends the first chapter with: "As a general rule, people, even the wicked, are much more naïve and simple-hearted than we suppose. And we ourselves are too."

Notice the humility.

*

The novel begins in a way I doubt Dostoyevski would've chosen had he lived in our faster, less patient times, with background of the characters and the conflicts in which they're embroiled. Not many pages after he accomplishes all that, he gives us Father Zossima, a saintly fellow whose only connection to the main plot of the novel is his influence over Alyosha Karamazov.

The Zossima scenes are so rich, I suspect they come direct from the Spirit, who provides the wisdom because Dostoyevski makes himself perfectly vulnerable. Through the buffoon Fyodor Karamazov, Dostoyevski's namesake, he confesses the most shameful parts of his own character.

The instigating question of the scene in which Fyodor visits Zossima is: what will happen between this degenerate buffoon and this saint? Then Fyodor (Karamazov/Dostoyevski) pours out the coarse, abusive, sniveling and foolish parts of his nature, not even humbly but through boasting, which adds to his shame.

Later, in the persona of another buffoon, Madame Khokhlakov, Dostoyevski begins revealing his doubts and lapses of faith in words that wouldn't come from

174

anyone who hadn't doubted.

In exchange for the author's honesty, the Spirit gives him Zossima's profound responses to the buffoons and to a cast of petitioners.

As they are many and best read in context, I refer you to the novel.

*

Whenever new characters appear and develop, Dostoyevski takes care to let their side of the story at least be implied. And when he gets to the lowliest of them, Captain Snegiryov (whom Dmitri Karamazov has humiliated) and the Captain's son Ilyusha, Dostoyevski's passion escalates. He appears to feel wounds the family suffered, an impossible task to any writer who hadn't felt, from experience or through inspired compassion, the scourge of being weak and poor and at the mercy of the rich and powerful.

Dostoyevski loves all his characters.

*

Ivan Karamazov talks to brother Alyosha about a trip to Europe and how he intends to "steep my soul in my emotion." He explains, "It's not a matter of intellect or logic, it's loving with one's inside, with one's guts."

And Alyosha, a monk, responds, "I think everyone should love life above everything in the world."

At church, when Warren Larkin welcomed people or prayed or whatever, he was like a flash flood of enthusiasm. I have observed Warren and wondered how he survives, he seems to live with his heart so close to the surface. It must get bashed regularly. He must be awfully strong.

I imagine Dostoyevski being like Warren. At his writing desk, he takes his heart out of his chest and puts it in full view, where the Spirit can readily feed it.

When Ivan counters Alyosha's faith with his virulent cynicism, we hear Dostoyevski arguing with himself.

Ivan begins with the most common argument against God, the injustices he sees. He gives plentiful and graphic examples of people's vicious attacks upon each other, even upon children. Then he admits, "I believe like a child that the suffering will be healed and made up for, that all the humiliating absurdity of human contradictions will vanish like a pitiful mirage, that in the world's finale, at the moment of eternal harmony, something so precious will come to pass that it will suffice for all hearts, for the comforting of all resentments, for the atonement of all the crimes of humanity, and the blood they've shed; that will make it not only possible to forgive but to justify all that has happened with men." Still, he refuses to trust. "But though all that may come to pass, I don't accept it. I won't accept it."

Alyosha is the author's heart and spirit with the mind subdued, while Ivan is Dostoyevski's mind with the spirit amputated.

"'I understand nothing,' Ivan went on, as though in delirium. 'I don't want to understand anything now. I want to stick to the fact. I made up my mind long ago not to understand. If I try to understand anything, I shall be false to the fact and I have determined to stick to the fact.'"

Ivan is the intellectual, probably the closest of the brothers to his creator. And this creed he expresses, the refusal to understand, is a secret of Dostoyevski's greatness. The artist had better explore, observe and report than imagine he fully understands a character or a society or the universe. When we think we fully understand, we have passed judgment. As a writer, in the perfect or near-perfect state Dostoyevski must have achieved before the Spirit would so generously feed him, he couldn't allow any opinion or dogma to bend or shape his vision of what he had observed.

Of course, if his observations are what have led to his view of the world and his beliefs, they should in the end prove out that view and belief system.

*

"The Grand Inquisitor" chapter, which I previously touched upon, is an exploration of the mystery we call freedom. The Inquisitor, after finding Jesus has come to visit earth, takes him captive and condemns him for setting people free.

He maintains that if, in the desert when tempted by "the wise and dread spirit," Christ had succumbed and turned stones into bread, he would've "satisfied the universal and everlasting craving of humanity individually and together as one — to find someone to worship."

And if Christ had taken the dread spirit's offer and cast himself off the cliff and counted upon angels to save him, by depending upon such a miracle to persuade the people, he would have relieved them of their ability to choose whether or not to believe. The Inquisitor argues, "For man seeks not so much God as the miraculous."

If Christ had accepted the offer to rule all the world, he would've given mankind everything it longs for. "That is, someone to worship [for the bread he provides], someone to keep his conscience [using the ammunition of miracle to persuade] and some means of uniting all in one unanimous and harmonious anthill [by ruling over them], for the craving for universal unity is the third and last anguish of men."

But Christ held firm, declined Satan's offers, and thereby granted and insured our freedom. So, the Inquisitor argues, Christ did humanity a tragic disservice, because only a precious few of us can bear freedom. As for the others: "Because we [of the Inquisition] are ready to endure the freedom which they have found to be dreadful and to rule over them, we shall persuade them that they will only become free when they renounce their freedom to us and submit to us."

Though methods of persuasion have gotten more subtle since the age of the *auto da fe,* the suspicious or cynical amongst us would hold that even today in America, the church, along with numerous commercial interests and institutions, still conspires to steal our freedom.

As the Inquisitor assures Jesus, most people can live without freedom.

Maybe most people can even thrive without freedom if they repress the artist within. But artists can't afford to turn their freedom over to a church, or to a totalitarian government, or to a publishing establishment addicted to the bottom line.

*

The sixth of the novel's twelve books is dedicated to presenting the beliefs of Father Zossima, the spiritual center of the story. After assuring our attention by hinting that Fyodor Karamazov will soon be murdered while leaving us to wonder who the murderer will be, Dostoyevski devotes several dozen pages to Zossima's life story, his vision for Russia and humankind.

"'We all are responsible to all for all, [and for all their sins] apart from our own sins. And in very truth, so soon as men understand that, the Kingdom of Heaven will be for them not a dream, but a living reality. Until you have become really, in actual fact, a brother to everyone, brotherhood will not come to pass. No sort of scientific teaching, no kind of common interest, will ever teach men to share property and privileges with equal consideration for all. Everyone will think his share too small and they will always envy, complain, and attack one another. But this terrible individualism must inevitably have an end, and all will understand how unnaturally they are separated from one another. It will be the spirit of the time, and people will marvel that they have sat so long in darkness without seeing the light. And then the sign of the Son of Man will be seen in the heavens.'"

Dostoyevski wants us to take this as more than an old monk's rant. Scholar and translator Ralph Matlaw writes, "The leading idea of the novel is that 'we are all responsible for everyone and everything.'"

No doubt, Dostoyevski realized most readers would find the concept strange and perhaps as alienating as Christ telling his disciples they would have to eat his flesh and drink his blood. Still, he risked making it the center of the novel about which he wrote to a friend "I would die happy if I could finish this final novel, for I would have expressed myself completely."

So he accepted the artistic risk and wrote with the intensity of a gambler who has bet on one hand the last of his money and all he could borrow.

*

On his death bed, Zossima says, "Fathers and teachers, forgive my tears now, for all my childhood rises up again before me, and I breathe now as I breathed then, with the breast of a little child of eight, and I feel as I did then, awe and wonder and gladness."

Remember, Christ tells us that to enter the Kingdom of Heaven we must become like little children. With that qualification in mind, let's suppose the place where the artist needs to go to hear without static the voice of the Spirit is a neighborhood in or on the outskirts of the Kingdom of Heaven. Then we must go there as children, free of stereotypes and preconceptions, able to look at the world, the beautiful and the sordid, with awe and fresh vision. To perceive God's creation in the newness of love, as Father Zossima advises: "Brothers, have no fear of men's sin. Love a man even in his sin, for that is the semblance of Divine Love and is the highest love on earth. Love all God's creation, the whole and every grain of sand in it. Love every leaf, every ray of God's light. Love the animals, love the plants, love everything. If you love everything, you will perceive the divine mystery in things."

Which means, if I desire to write more remarkable stuff, I must learn to love better.

Long ago, I reasoned that if I learned more about love, I could hope to discover more about God. So I set out to read everything I could about love.

The study of love is so crucial to our spiritual growth, if we dedicate ourselves to the process, the Spirit will guide us to the sources.

*

Without guidance from the Spirit, Dostoyevski couldn't have written Dmitri's confession with its soul searching and paradoxes, its exposure of the complexity of his heart and mind, in which every reader should recognize his own heart and mind and begin to pardon himself for his failures and transgressions, as he pardons Dmitri.

He couldn't have written that confession without becoming Dmitri, giving himself over totally to his character even at the risk of his sanity. To do justice to his creation, required offering himself as a sacrifice.

The story closest to the hearts of us Christians tells of God becoming human and sacrificing himself for the sake of his creations. So if we have the nerve to consider ourselves creators, should we expect the Spirit to guide us if we aren't willing to sacrifice for our creations like God did for his?

In Tae Kwon Do, before we tested for the black belt, Master Jeong asked if we were willing to die while testing. Because, he said, "If you are not willing to die, do not fight or you will lose." We writers need to ask ourselves, "Are you willing to search for and report on the darkest as well as the brightest places in your heart and mind, even if you sense terror in the dark or the light starts to blind you?" If not, you won't write a masterpiece.

Every experience, actual or vicarious, changes us. As we become our characters, live with them and learn from them, our understanding broadens. And as our understanding grows, if we're true to ourselves, our stories change.

*

In *The Brothers Karamazov*, we find Dmiitri asking a carriage driver if he [Dmitri] will go to hell. The driver answers, "You're like a little child. That's how we look on you. And though you're hasty tempered, sir, yet God will forgive you for your kind heart."

Dostoyevski's insistence on this theme indicates he sought, or had found and known the beauty of, such forgiveness for his own excesses. And belief in such forgiveness freed him from the guilt and consequent restraint or timidity that limits the access of many writers to the spirit that moves us.

*

In Book 10, "The Boys," the characters are each so uniquely human they demonstrate the clarity with which Dostoyevski observed speech, gestures, actions, and the depths of the minds and hearts that caused the actions. Even his minor characters live and breathe as creatures so distinct and unique, they at least begin to help us grasp why God loves us all.

Inspiration usually comes to those who also exercise their imaginations and their powers of observation. W.B. Yeats noted that to deliver their messages, the spirits need to use our minds and our powers of observation. In *The Brothers Karamazov*,

Fetyukovich, the famous orator and lawyer from St. Petersburg tells us, "A thousand things may happen in reality which elude even the subtlest imagination." As though hearkening to the implications of his lawyer character's remark, Dostoyevski watches, listens, and builds out of details he has observed.

All of the Karamazov brothers, each time they appear, exhibit new complexities. Dmitri, in his final scene, when his heart and mind lie exposed, becomes a masterpiece of consistency. Every decision he makes, every action and thought feels earned, prepared for. All the impetuous passions, the insecurity and bitterness, the generous and cruel actions, piece together into as complex yet convincing a person as fiction offers.

Though minor characters appear in less detail, still they are vivid, unique and peculiar while remaining true to life. So with Kolya, the leader of the boys, we not only know he's a peculiarly smart thirteen-year-old, rather spoiled by his mother and idolized by his fellow students, but also that he loves smaller children and playing their games but is secretive about this weakness that doesn't match his self image. We know he's lonely and troubled by the need to answer adult questions he hasn't lived enough to answer except by drawing on other people's ideas.

We know Kolya often suffers from feeling ridiculous. So Alyosha advises him never to concern himself about appearing ridiculous, since worrying about looking ridiculous is a malady clever people are prone to.

At the risk of belaboring, I'll argue that we clever writers ought to heed Alyosha's advice, quit worrying and risk feeling ridiculous. Because the two greatest crimes against the spirit that moves us may be the unwillingness to look ridiculous and the timidity that keep us from writing what might be heretical according to church or social dogma.

*

At the book's end, Dostoyevski refuses to give us anything like perfect closure. We don't have any promise about what's to become of Dmitri or his women, or his brother Ivan. Though the novel is certainly melodrama, and melodrama generally calls for closure, Dostoyevski insists on the truth, that every victory is tainted by some grief. Still, though he concludes with the novel's most tragic scene, on the last page he lifts our spirits by pointing us to the only way we can triumph over bitterness, misery, despair or evil. His ending is a call for love and hope, as all endings would be in the world I suggest we should strive for, even at the risk of suffering, or of appearing childlike or ridiculous.

seven — Notes About Sources

Since I'm neither a scholar nor a plagiarist, I'm simply going to list the books in which I found quotes and ideas that helped me create this collection.

Feodor Dostoyevski, a biography by Alba Amoia that brought me closer to understanding the great novelist.

The Norton Critical Edition of *The Brothers Karamazov*, which presents a wide selection of criticism as well as historical background and letters of the author that enrich the experience of reading Dostoyevski.

Edward Hirsch's excellent *The Angel and the Demon*, which uses the work and lives of poets and other artists in the search for the source of artistic inspiration, and which informed my allusions to Charles Baudelaire, Ralph Waldo Emerson, Karl Jung, Garcia Lorca, Ranier Maria Rilke, Charles Simic, and William Butler Yeats.

Mystery and Manners, a miscellany of prose by Flannery O'Connor, which offers a wealth of her observations and musings about the place of the Christian writer.

William Kaufman's *Existentialism from Dostoyevski to Sartre*, in which I found passages from Kierkegaard and Nietzsche that spoke to my quest for better understanding of how and why the spirit works.

Going on Faith, edited by William Zinnser, in which a variety of authors give their views on writing as a spiritual quest, and from which I gleaned ideas from Allen Ginsberg and Frederick Buechner.

And various editions of *The Holy Bible* have provided enough wisdom and mystery to keep me thinking and learning forever.

Whoever needs more detail on any of the books and can't find it on the web should email me at: ken@kenkuhlken.net. I'll try to help.

by SUSAN SALGUERO:

The Gachi. She wasn't the only angry woman at U.C. Berkeley. Always on edge but unaware why, she knew she had to flee. A passion for music delivered her to Spain. There she staked her life on Flamenco.

by JARED BROWN:

Million Dollar Man. A phone call from a neighbor reporting a suspicious character at his home sends Jared Brown, a family man and Christian psychologist, to the outskirts of hell.

by ALAN RUSSELL & KEN KUHLKEN:

No Cats, No Chocolate. Mystery authors launch an adventure with high hopes and dreams of winning the fame they're convinced they deserve, as guests on a national television show. ~ An Amazon #1 bestseller in several categories.

by OLGA SAVITSKY:

Shockabonda. Writers often imagine their ideal reader and compose accordingly. The reader Olga Savitsky

189

chose was God. Since she wasn't likely to fool her reader, she needed to be real.

by KEN KUHLKEN:

Midheaven. High school senior Jodi McGee turns from drugs and boys to Christ, but soon thereafter falls for her English teacher. As a result, tragedies test her will, her faith, and her sanity. ~Finalist for PEN's Ernest Hemingway Award for best first novel.

Reading Brother Lawrence. During a troubled time, novelist Ken Kuhlken discovered a certain book helped him find peace. *Reading Brother Lawrence* chronicles his search for understanding.

Write Smart. Much acclaimed author Ken Kuhlken shares insights gained over thirty-some years as a novelist, university creative writing professor, and founder of Perelandra College. By following the Write Smart process, writers will efficiently create, revise, and sell their stories.

by NICOLE L RIVERA:

Finding Unauthorized Faith in Harry Potter. Nicole L Rivera, Creative Team Manager for the fansite

MuggleNet, marries faith with fandom in this wise and compelling devotional. Drawing on the Harry Potter story and parallels from the Bible, she reflects upon life's deepest truths, about faith, friendship, courage, loyalty, and love, and provides us with the keys to living like Christ and the Harry Potter heroes.

Hickey's Books provides support for the Perelandra College writing programs in the effort to enrich popular literature and writers' lives. Learn more at: **perelandra.edu**

BE A CALIFORNIA EXPERT

The Tom Hickey crime novels are riveting stories that also offer a vivid and panoramic vision of California as it transforms from a frontier to the most influential place on earth.

"Elegant, eloquent, and elegiac, Kuhlken's novels sing an old melody, at the same time haunting and beautiful." Don Winslow, author of The Cartel

Readers who accompany Tom and his extraordinary family on their adventures enrich their knowledge of history and the dark and bright recesses of the human heart.

"Tom Hickey is one of detective fiction's most original and intriguing creations." San Francisco Chronicle

The Biggest Liar in Los Angeles: L.A. 1926. Tom is a young bandleader when a family friend gets lynched in Echo Park. ~ A San Diego Book Awards Best Mystery.

The Good Know Nothing: L.A., Tucson, McCloud, 1936. New evidence sends L.A. police detective Tom on a search for his father, who vanished long ago. ~ **A** Los Angeles Book Festival Best Mystery

The Venus Deal: San Diego, Mount Shasta, Denver, Tijuana, 1942. Tom is a partner in a supper club when he discovers that a gifted jazz singer he employs has contracted for a murder

.

The Loud Adios: San Diego, Tijuana, 1943. While serving as an M.P. on the Mexican border, Tom learns of German and Mexican Nazi plotting in Tijuana. ~ St. Martins Press, Private Eye Writers of America Best First P.I. Novel

The Angel Gang: Lake Tahoe, San Diego, Los Angeles, 1950. When L.A. and Las Vegas mobs invade Lake Tahoe, Tom's pregnant wife Wendy gets taken hostage.

The Do-Re-Mi: Rural Northern California, 1971. The Hickey's adopted son Alvaro, a musician booked at a folk festival, flees from a murder accusation. ~ A Shamus Best Novel.

The Vagabond Virgins: San Diego, Rural Baja California, 1979. A heavenly apparition appears in Baja California rallying the faithful to overthrow the corrupt ruling party.

Visit **kenkuhlken.net** for special offers.

ABOUT THE AUTHOR

Ken Kuhlken's stories have appeared in *Esquire* and dozens of other magazines and anthologies, been honorably mentioned in *Best American Short Stories*, and earned a National Endowment for the Arts Fellowship. He has been a frequent contributor and a columnist for the *San Diego Reader.*

His novels are *Midheaven*, a finalist for the Ernest Hemingway Award for best first novel: and the Tom Hickey California crime novels.

With Alan Russell, in *Road Kill* and *No Cats, No Chocolate,* he has chronicled the madness of book tours. In *Writing and the Spirit* he offers a wealth of advice to writers and everyone looking for inspiration. *Reading Brother Lawrence* follows him on a spiritual quest.

He resides on the web at: **kenkuhlken.net**

CPSIA information can be obtained
at www.ICGtesting.com
Printed in the USA
FSOW02n0618100118
42912FS

9 780996 524285